T0128858

.

The Road To Helsinki

The Road To Helsinki

An Analysis of European International Relations Leading to The Conference on Security and Cooperation in Europe

A Thesis presented to the Graduate Faculty of the University of Virginia
By John Guilford Kerr
In Candidacy for the Degree of Master of Arts
Woodrow Wilson Department of Government and Foreign Affairs
University of Virginia
August 1977

THE ROAD TO HELSINKI
AN ANALYSIS OF EUROPEAN INTERNATIONAL
RELATIONS LEADING TO THE CONFERENCE ON
SECURITY AND COOPERATION IN EUROPE

iUniverse books may be ordered through booksellers or by contacting:

iUniverse
1663 Liberty Drive
Bloomington, IN 47403
www.iuniverse.com
1-800-Authors (1-800-288-4677)

Because of the dynamic nature of the Internet, any web addresses or links contained in this book may have changed since publication and may no longer be valid. The views expressed in this work are solely those of the author and do not necessarily reflect the views of the publisher, and the publisher hereby disclaims any responsibility for them.

Any people depicted in stock imagery provided by Thinkstock are models, and such images are being used for illustrative purposes only. Certain stock imagery © Thinkstock.

ISBN: 978-1-4917-6921-8 (sc)
ISBN: 978-1-4917-6922-5 (e)

Library of Congress Control Number: 2015908548

Print information available on the last page.

iUniverse rev. date: 6/17/2015

Contents

Preface to the 2015 Publication

When I wrote <u>The Road To Helsinki</u>, it was intended to be not only an analysis of how the idea of a pan-European security conference evolved, but also as an advocacy for U.S. participation in the conference. I chose this thesis topic in the summer of 1976, one year after the Final Act was signed. American participation was still being hotly debated, and many among my colleagues and the faculty of the Department of Government and Foreign affairs at the University of Virginia opposed U.S. participation. Critiques of the Conference ranged from that it was simply unnecessary, to the contention that a conference that had been long advocated by the U.S.S.R. would do nothing but secure Soviet domination of Eastern Europe and provide a platform for meddling in Western Europe. I believed that both the political process that led to the Conference on Security and Cooperation in Europe, as well as the provisions in the Final Act, would act as a slow corrosive on the authoritarian regimes in Eastern Europe. I felt strongly that the formal endorsement by the heads of government of the Principles enumerated in the Final Act of the CSCE, even though it was not legally binding under international law, would gradually lead toward greater cooperation between Eastern and Western Europe, that it would foster democratic reforms and economic development in the countries of Eastern Europe, and that it would lead ultimately to a reduction of Soviet influence, not more.

The Final Act of the CSCE was signed on August 1, 1975, almost thirty years to the day since the atomic bomb was dropped on Hiroshima. For the fortieth anniversary of the signing of the Final Act, I thought it would be appropriate to republish this history of how the Conference came into being. In rereading the story, I might well have called it "The Conference That Almost Wasn't". The perseverance of countless diplomats and politicians from thirty-five countries made the CSCE happen. Most of the players have long since left the stage, but they deserve to be remembered for their efforts in ending the Cold War.

The forty years since the Final Act was signed have not been without strife in Europe: martial law in Poland in 1981, the Balkan war in the 1990s after the break-up of Yugoslavia, and today's conflict between the Russian Federation and Ukraine. The "standing institution" that was under consideration in order to continue the work of the Conference had not yet been created in 1977. The Organization for Security and Cooperation ("OSCE") was officially established in 1994. The OSCE has been in the news recently for its role in trying to mediate the conflict in the Ukraine. But the changes in Europe since August 1975: the reunification of Germany, the dissolution of the U.S.S.R, the expansion of NATO and the EU, have justified the hopes of those who advocated U.S. participation in the CSCE. There are few straight lines between cause and effect in history, but it is clear that warnings by the critics of the Conference have not come true. It is tempting to say about the dogged Soviet advocacy for the Conference, "Be careful what you wish for." But the CSCE has also improved the security and economic development of the former members of the Soviet Union and the countries of Eastern Europe, even though the Warsaw Pact, the U.S.S.R., and Comecon no longer exist.

Today, many of the words and phrases in <u>The Road To Helsinki,</u> such as "East-West", "Cold War", "blocs", and "détente" sound anachronistic. I believe the Conference on Security and Cooperation was important in moving Europe beyond the divisions that had separated Europe into armed camps since the end of World War Two.

To close this preface and begin the story, it seems appropriate to end with a quote attributed to Winston Churchill at a White House luncheon on June 26th in 1956*, about the same time that the idea of a pan-European conference was first raised. Mr. Churchill was reported to have remarked:

"To jaw-jaw is always better than to war-war."

John Guilford Kerr
Kailua Kona, Hawaii
April 2015

---

* Four months earlier, on February 25th, 1956 at the twentieth congress of the Communist Party of the Soviet Union - the first since the death of Josef Stalin in 1953 - Nikita Khrushchev, First Secretary of the Party, denounced Stalin and 'The Personality Cult and its Consequences'. Four months later, on November 4th, 1956 the Warsaw Pact invaded Hungary.

Introduction

On August 1, 1975 thirty-three European states and the United States and Canada met in Helsinki, Finland to sign the Final Act of the Conference on Security and Cooperation in Europe (CSCE). Among the communist states the document was hailed as a milestone in European international relations. Eastern analysts stressed that after thirty years of obstinacy the Western states had finally recognized the legitimacy of the post-war borders in Europe and they had disavowed any attempts to change those borders by force or by subverting the communist regimes in Eastern Europe. Western opinion of the agreement signed at Helsinki was divided. Officially, the governments of the Western states approved the Final Act of the CSCE. They described it as a step in the process of détente and they pointed with satisfaction to the provision forbidding the use of force in European international relations. In particular, Western proponents argued that the section of the Final Act dealing with human rights would improve the human condition of millions of East Europeans oppressed by their governments. If those governments did not allow more freedom for their citizens as called for in the Final Act, then, the CSCE proponents argued, the West would have the document as a tangible basis from which to criticize the Eastern regimes. However, many Western observers labeled the Helsinki agreements as a "sell-out" of the East European states to Soviet hegemony since the agreements seemed to imply that the West formally accepted the Soviet control over the regimes in those states. From this point of view the West should have had much more in the way of tangible changes in the relations between East and West, such as in arms control, rather than symbolic expressions of intent of human rights before agreeing to the Final Act.

The thesis supported in this study is that Western states made the correct decision in adopting a positive attitude toward the CSCE, that the process of détente which led to Western acceptance of the CSCE proposal was beneficial to Western interests and European security generally, and that the CSCE itself opened up new possibilities for East-West cooperation.

Of course, there were risks for both sides in the process of détente just as there were risks for both sides during the years of the Cold War. Western confrontations with "monolithic communism" from Berlin to Korea convinced the West of the implacability of the Soviet threat. NATO was created to meet that threat. When West Germany was formally included in the NATO alliance the communist countries created the Warsaw Pact in response. The relations between the communist and non-communist halves of Europe became frozen into a "logic of confrontation" against which events and policies were evaluated. The danger of the situation was that it magnified small frictions between the blocs thus encouraging mutual paranoia and an expensive arms race. Ironically however, the atmosphere of confrontation also had the effect of stabilizing the chaotic post-war political situation in Europe, particularly in relation to Germany. From the stability conferred by the opposed alliances the two sides eventually felt safe enough to look out from behind their defenses. They gradually became more confident that carefully controlled contacts and negotiations with each other would not risk a dangerous change in the status quo.

1. *The creation of a status quo, set in a formal context of East-West confrontation, provided the basis for ending those hostilities that were founded on a lack of certainty about the manner in which political relations of the Continent were to be ordered. But in achieving this status quo through a specifically military alliance, the nations concerned with Europe's security imposed a logic of confrontation that had to be followed through, step by step, until there was a strategic stability in Europe to match the political stability conferred by the very act of establishing the two blocs.* [1]

The logic of confrontation was followed through in a series of "freezes" and "thaws" in East-West relations during the 1950s and early 1960s. The West believed that the death of Stalin might lower the Soviet threat to their security as well as lead to some liberalization of Soviet society. To some extent this proved to be true. Khrushchev was generally believed to be a moderate in his international and domestic policies compared to the old Stalinists in the Soviet leadership. For example, Khrushchev revised the time-honored dogma of communist theory that war between the communist and capitalist states was inevitable. Instead he advocated "peaceful coexistence" and economic competition between the blocs until capitalism collapsed by itself. This change was greeted favorably, if somewhat suspiciously, by the West.

It was during a thaw in East-West relations in 1954-1956, early in Khrushchev's period of leadership, that the forerunners of the CSCE proposals of the late 1960s are found. The Soviet Union and its East European allies suggested several ideas for dismantling the military blocs and instituting a pan-European security scheme. Included in these suggestions were proposed solutions to the German question. Eastern intent behind the proposals was to prevent the potentially powerful West Germans from being irrevocably joined to the opposing military alliance. For the West, acceptance of the Eastern proposals would have meant leaving all of Germany open to Soviet subversion.

These first proposals for some form of pan-European organization died quickly in the atmosphere of Cold War. The Soviet invasion of Hungary in 1956 ended the thaw in East-West relations. The concurrent Suez Crisis which divided the Western alliance was a harbinger of future problems for NATO cohesion. These events reasserted the logic of confrontation and killed Khrushchev's "peace offensive". His policy came under increasing attack from other Politburo members and although he defeated the "anti-party group" in 1957, his policy toward Europe and the West generally was marked throughout the rest of his period of leadership by extreme inconsistency as he alternately rattled rockets and preached peaceful coexistence.

For NATO, the danger of internal arguments weakening the alliance became the primary source of concern when analyzing the Eastern pan-European security proposals. If the Soviet Union could convince even a few of the NATO countries that their security interests would be better served in a pan-European organization rather than by two opposing alliances it would threaten the security of all the NATO countries. Most importantly, it was clear to Western analysts that the U.S.S.R. wanted American influence in Europe to decline, to be replaced by Soviet influence. Until 1970 the Eastern proposals for a European security conference would exclude the United States from participation, or at best be very ambiguous about the role of the U.S. in future European security arrangements.

Charles de Gaulle's policy of reasserting French independence of action in foreign affairs added to the concerns of the other NATO countries that their alliance might be losing its credibility as a deterrent to Soviet aggression and therefore, as a counter-balance to the political weight of Soviet military strength. However, by the time that de Gaulle formally withdrew France from the military aspects of NATO, a new certainty in the European military and political balance was producing a relaxation of tensions that mitigated the fears that a French withdrawal would have produced ten years earlier.

Part of the certainty involved more clear-cut and accurate perceptions for both the East and West of what the other side would fight for. The Berlin airlift, the invasion of Hungary, the erection of the Berlin Wall, and the Cuban missile crisis were important events in the mutual learning process. Along with the territorial certainty, by the early 1960s the balance of strategic nuclear weapons began to make it clear to both alliances that allowing tensions to lead to war risked mutual annihilation. That realization was an extremely important inducement to find some form of cooperation to avoid confrontations that could escalate into war.

Just as the NATO alliance was concerned about its cohesion, so the U.S.S.R. was concerned by the growing rift with China. By the early 1960s that rift had become public and vituperative. The superpowers sought to mitigate the threat of alliance instability and the danger of nuclear war by finding ways of easing tensions in their bilateral relationship on one hand and preaching vigilance to allies on the other. Agreements were signed by the U.S. and the U.S.S.R. in 1963 for a "hot line" between Washington and Moscow and on a limited test ban treaty. At the same time NATO was searching for methods of nuclear sharing, which worried the Soviets, and the Soviet Union took care to renew its bilateral treaty ties with the East Europeans.

Essentially what was happening was a change in the perception of the risks inherent in cooperating with the other side. The problems facing both alliances, alliance cohesion and vulnerability to nuclear attack, were gradually reshaping their "danger priorities" and their attitudes toward détente – ultimately toward the CSCE. The superpowers wanted détente but they did not want that détente to affect, as far as Europe was concerned, the elements of power at their disposal. [2]

For the Soviet Union the CSCE proposal had many potential advantages. Since the suggestion at least appeared to be in a spirit of cooperation and conciliation, it was good propaganda to be able to accuse the West of dragging its feet in the quest for normalizing East-West relations when NATO ignored the CSCE proposals. By appearing to be faithfully seeking détente with their proposal, the Soviets might have hoped that the West Europeans would begin to perceive a declining Soviet menace and lower their defense expenditures. Such a development might also slow the progress toward West European integration and make Western Europe's connections with the U.S. appear less vital. If the CSCE idea came to fruition, the Soviets may have believed, the American military presence in Europe might be eliminated, clearing the way for increased Soviet influence in West European politics. A CSCE was planned as a forum in which the G.D.R., the U.S.S.R.'s most important trading partner and ally, would at last be given full recognition by the West as a legitimate state. If the CSCE produced agreement on the permanency of existing borders in Europe it would repudiate West German non-recognition of the Oder-Neisse boundary and the boundary between the two Germanys. If the CSCE were successful in scaling down the threat from the West, it would allow the Soviet Union to shift more resources to the increasingly volatile border with China. Finally, the prospect of more access to Western technology and capital coming from a CSCSE weighed in Soviet calculations.

Some of these motivations were also held by the other members of the Warsaw Pact. There were some differences. The East Europeans are rankled to some degree by the political hegemony of the Soviet Union. In the CSCE idea they may have seen an opportunity for asserting more independence in both domestic and foreign policy. The fact that this motivation is in direct opposition to the supposed Soviet motivation of gaining "legitimization" of its hegemony through the CSCE, points to the divergent motivations held by the U.S.S.R. and its allies, yet all advocated a pan-European conference.

To speak of Western motivations for the CSCE in the early 1960s is somewhat misleading. The West at that time was naturally highly suspicious of a proposal so strongly advocated by the U.S.S.R. That general skepticism was evident even during the Conference. Western analysts were aware of the potential benefits a CSCE held for the Soviet Union. The strategy NATO developed in response to the rather embarrassing CSCE proposal was to insist on concrete evidence that the U.S.S.R. was committed to normalizing East-West relations. However, solutions to the outstanding issues, such as recognition of the G.D.R., the territorial questions, and the status of Berlin, were out of reach as long as the F.R.G. remained intransigent and was backed by the rest of NATO. By the mid-1960s under the Erhard government, and even more under the Grand Coalition led by Kiesinger, the F.R.G. began to approach the East European states through trade agreements, but the policy was aimed at isolating the G.D.R. and it was countered by the U.S.S.R. The United States tried to pursue a similar policy toward the East Europeans. Described as "bridge-building" by the Johnson administration, the policy was aimed at low level agreements but their effect did not spill over into the more sensitive areas that most concerned the U.S.S.R.

If the Soviet Union had stopped the growth of economic, cultural, and scientific contacts that constituted "bridge-building", it would have indicated that they were not sincere in their appeals for pan-European cooperation. That they permitted the contacts indicated at least that the leadership was not overly concerned with the growing permeability of the Iron Curtain. In the mid-1960s the new Soviet leadership travelled to many of the West European capitals on missions of friendship. From 1965 until the invasion Czechoslovakia in 1968, Western opinion was slowly being convinced that the Soviet Union was sincere in their efforts at détente and the CSCE proposal began to gain the support of some neutral countries as well as more appreciation from the NATO countries. American participation remained at issue however, and that question stalled the momentum toward the CSCE.

The United States was preoccupied with the war in Vietnam, a war with the look of international communist aggression, and the West Europeans moved ahead of the Americans in the development of détente in Europe. The economic exchanges and extension of human contacts in the mid-1960s also had a greater impact on the West Europeans than on the U.S. and this too made them more favorable to détente. The United States recognized the need to formulate some positive détente strategy of its own for Europe. It was also important to rally all of NATO around the strategy. To counter the CSCE proposal, NATO explicitly named several areas where negotiations should be conducted first to see if a basis really existed for a valuable CSCE. Those areas were Berlin, relations between the two Germanys, strategic arms control, and later, force reductions in Europe. The position of the F.R.G. leadership was crucial to the fulfillment of these conditions.

Chapter One of this study examines the period from the ascension to power of Brezhnev in 1964 to mid-1970 when NATO officially accepted the CSCE idea, subject to the completion of the four-power Berlin negotiations with the East. It was also in mid-1970 when the Warsaw Pact explicitly accepted North American participation in the CSCE. Brezhnev made the CSCE the cornerstone of his policy toward Europe. The Warsaw Pact's "Declaration of Strengthening Peace and Security in Europe" issued from Bucharest in July 1966 brought the CSCE proposal to the fore-front of Soviet policy. It was countered by the West for the next four years by requests that the substantive issues be dealt with first. Chapter One examines the process of communication between the blocs, and bilaterally, particularly by the F.R.G., to find the points at issue, the positions taken, and how those positions gradually changed. These changes were the result of new perceptions of risks, abilities, and possibilities.

Most importantly, the invasion of Czechoslovakia is assessed in Chapter One for its impact on the CSCE proposal. That invasion was also a communication from the U.S.S.R. that indicated that the Soviets would only negotiate from the situation of "certainty" in which détente had grown. The Western reaction to the invasion, best exemplified by the "Ostpolitik" of Willy Brandt in 1969, was crucial to the CSCE proposal.

Chapter Two describes the outcomes of negotiations which NATO had made prerequisites for the CSCE. Did these negotiations provide the tangible evidence of Soviet sincerity which NATO wanted? Did they improve security in Europe and did they improve the human conditions for residents of Berlin and Germany? Chapter Two supports an affirmative response to these questions. The result came in the form of Warsaw Pact agreement to discuss force reductions in Central Europe in parallel with the CSCE. It was also evidenced by the SALT I Agreement.

All of these successful negotiations set the stage for the CSCE. The fact that these mutually satisfactory agreements could be achieved indicated to the West that perhaps some further progress in détente could come from a carefully planned CSCE. Since the West had held the negotiations noted above as prerequisites for the CSCE, the Conference was valuable as the inducement for Soviet participation in the negotiations. However, NATO went to the CSCE with the positive attitude of making the negotiations in the Conference itself beneficial to Western interests, rather than simply participating lethargically or obstructively. NATO participation at the CSCE was more than just payment for Soviet concessions in previous negotiations.

The last half of Chapter Two deals with the negotiations in the CSCE and with the product of those negotiations, the Final Act. The negotiations lasted more than two years and the Final Act represents compromises by all of the states involved. Perhaps the most important aspect of the Final Act examined in Chapter Two is the Basket III section concerning human rights. NATO implicitly adopted this issue as the quid pro quo for its agreement on the sections dealing with military security, inviolability of frontiers, and economic cooperation. Many people in the West will judge the ultimate "usefulness" of the CSCE by Eastern compliance with the provisions concerning human rights in the Final Act.

Over the years, as the political atmosphere changed from Cold War to détente, the attitudes of the countries in NATO and the Warsaw Pact toward the CSCE proposal also changed. The Soviet Union might have maintained some hope for unilateral advantage from the CSCE in terms of influence in Western Europe, but those hopes became remote as the East Europeans showed an interest in having the CSCE invalidate the Brezhnev doctrine and NATO began insisting on human rights as an area of first-rank importance in the Conference negotiations. The West, at first intending only to use the CSCE proposal as a carrot to lead the U.S.S.R. into other negotiations, later found the Conference to be an inviting area for further testing Soviet intentions. The advances in the technology of warfare which accrued to both sides in the 1950s and 1960s and which continue today were an impetus to finding ways of cooperating for mutual security. Force appears to lose its utility when it becomes mutually suicidal. Somewhat distracted by events in other parts of the world and disturbed by the unsteadiness of their alliances, the super powers looked to the frozen situation in Europe as an area where low-risk agreements could be made which might promote mutual security even though they continued to confront each other elsewhere. The economic and environmental benefits which could result from normalizing East-West relations as well as the possibility of slowing the arms race all militated for deepening détente in Europe. The proposals in the 1950s by the U.S.S.R. for a pan-European solution to the division of Europe were formulated in the context of confrontation. The proposals were seldom equitable and usually punctuated by ideological tirades. Within the context of détente, which means a context of changing risk perception and changing national interests, resulting in more compatible foreign policies, the CSCE proposal itself changed as did Western attitudes toward the idea. Into this fluid situation came two relatively new leadership groups in 1964 with the election of Johnson in the United States and the removal of Khrushchev from power in the U.S.S.R.

CHAPTER I

Communication in Détente 1966-1970, Invasions and Invitations

As with the transition from the Kennedy administration to the Johnson administration, there was also a notable continuity in foreign policy toward Europe under the new Soviet leadership. Although in many ways their tactics differed from those of Khrushchev, less vituperation and bravado, the "gray bureaucrats" Brezhnev and Kosygin continued to seek détente with the Americans while taking advantage of opportunities to lessen American influence in Western Europe. For example, troop reductions in Central Europe were becoming an increasingly sensitive issue among the NATO allies in the relatively relaxed atmosphere of the mid-1960s. McNamara's "flexible response" strategy was part of this controversy. To exploit the NATO planning and burden sharing problems, Khrushchev in February 1963 presented a detailed draft of a non-aggression pact including troop reductions for confidence building to the Eighteen Nation Disarmament Committee of the United Nations (which had been established in 1962). Although the draft was unacceptable to the West, the Soviet Union continued this approach under the new leadership in December 1964 with a memorandum calling for troop reductions in Europe, for refraining from stationing nuclear weapons in West or East Germany, and for setting up observation posts inside the NATO and Warsaw Pact countries.[3] In the same month the Polish Foreign Minister Rapacki proposed again a European security conference, another concept which was first promulgated under Khrushchev.

The West perceived there suggestions as attempts at making NATO's problems with nuclear sharing and force reductions more difficult. Those problems were aggravated by a growing U.S. desire to reach some agreement with the Soviets on strategic arms limitations. American experts argued that it was essential for the U.S. to maintain ultimate control over the entire NATO military apparatus in Western Europe in order to balance during negotiations the unquestioned Soviet domination of their military bloc. However, the Europeans were unwilling to support financially a military power that increased only American diplomatic leverage. [4] In January 1965 the Political and Consultative Committee of the Warsaw Pact met in Warsaw. It was the first meeting of the Committee since July, 1963. The communique issued from the meeting called for a conference of European states to discuss measures for collective security in Europe. Here was another example of the continuity in foreign policy from Khrushchev to the new leadership. It was the continuing attempt to use the pan-European conference scheme to exclude the U.S. from a new European security system. One tactical change was evident, and that was the dropping of Khrushchev's attempts in the early 1960s to warm up relations with the Federal Republic of Germany. This was signaled by the abusive language applied to the West German "revanchists." Despite this change, the Soviets did not make any attempt to reopen the Berlin can of worms. It is likely that the main purpose of their attack on the F.R.G. was to refurbish the "German threat" as a cohesive for Eastern solidarity. This approach appeared necessary to the U.S.S.R. in light of the cautious but persistent approaches to the East Germans by the Erhard government in Bonn and the increasing internal unrest in several Soviet satellites. Romania in particular, after issuing its "declaration of independence" in March, 1964, manifested the desire for a freer hand in developing its relations with Western Europe.

One gets the distinct impression that during the mid-1960s the Soviet leaders were searching for some way to alleviate their concerns over Germany's future military power. However, they were uncertain how to neutralize that threat without being too conciliatory toward the "revanchists" and thereby giving the East Europeans the idea that they too might normalize relations with the F.R.G. Bonn made things difficult in early 1965 by scheduling a meeting of the Bundestag in West Berlin for March. The Bundestag had met regularly in Berlin from 1955 through 1958 but the practice had been stopped because of Khrushchev's unpredictable hostility toward the meetings. In 1965 the Soviets were "forced" to harass access routes to West Berlin in order to prevent this propaganda "victory" by the F.R.G. A crisis was avoided when the Bundestag meetings were cancelled.

Despite these irritations the Soviets received the West German Foreign Minister Carstens in Moscow in September 1965 thus demonstrating Russian interest in quiet talks with the F.R.G. The Soviets realized they were in danger of letting the initiative slip to the West Germans who had been slowly building up their image in the East under the direction of Foreign Minister Schroder. By the time of the Carstens visit, the F.R.G. had established trade missions in Romania, Poland, Hungary, and Bulgaria. Soviet-F.R.G. trade was already at a half a billion dollars annually. After the Carstens visit the Russians resumed their public anti-German tactics, hoping to use a non-proliferation treaty then under discussion with the U.S. to preclude the acquisition of nuclear weapons by the F.R.G.

Although the West German initiatives toward the East were most significant in light of their marked departure from the policy followed by Adenauer, it is important to realize that other West European states were also looking East. Of course, as I have mentioned, de Gaulle was interested in better relations with the U.S.S.R. and the East Europeans particularly after the new Erhard government in Bonn made it clear they would not let the F.R.G. play a supporting role in France's anti-American campaign. To the Soviet's delight, President de Gaulle called on Europeans at a press conference in February, 1965 to "envisage first examining together, then settling in common and lastly guaranteeing conjointly the solution to the question which is essentially that of their continent."[5] De Gaulle was always careful not to completely burn his bridges however, and he never excluded the Americans explicitly from a European settlement, asserting only that it must be the Europeans who take the first steps toward that settlement.

Britain too, staunchest of America's allies, was in on the Eastern de-marche. Foreign Secretary Michael Stewart visited Prague and Warsaw in 1965 but he would not stray far from the old line. The visits were primarily symbolic. For instance, Stewart would not agree to the Czech demand that the 1936 Munich Agreement be declared null and void *ab initio*. He based his rejection on the argument that to reject the infamous agreement from its initiation as illegal would jeopardize the sanctity of treaties generally, setting a dangerous precedent for binding agreements among nations. [6]

The West Europeans seemed to be more ambitious in their openings to the East from 1964 on, but with the possible exception of de Gaulle, America's allies were not going very far away from the American policy of "peaceful engagement". From 1964 through 1966 the U.S. developed the concept of "bridge building" to selected East European countries. The strategy was to explicitly disavow any intention of subverting the regimes of the East Europeans while tacitly assuming that increased contacts between East and West would strengthen the autonomy of the East Europeans. [7] It was believed within the American State Department that this subtle tactic would be less easily repulsed by the U.S.S.R. because it did not appear as openly aggressive as earlier "containment" or "roll back" strategies had. However, even this policy of selected ties with the East, which Averell Harriman said was meant to produce "a progressive loosening of external authority over Eastern European countries and the continuing assertion of national autonomy and diversity," met with opposition in the communist countries as well as from elements in the West. [8] Not surprisingly, the Soviets condemned the policy as merely a sophisticated form of the old "roll back" strategy. The American Congress also offered some opposition to the policy. Influenced by the mounting difficulties in Vietnam, the Congress was less adept at differentiating between the diversity within and the approaches to world-wide communism than was the State Department.

It appeared that the Western nations were generally heading in the same direction. The problem was one of coordinating policies so that the U.S.S.R. could not exploit individual differences. Many ideas were presented toward this end. For example, Henry Kissinger argued in 1966 that diplomacy which could lead to the reunification of Europe must be kept separate from that which concerned the defense of Europe. He suggested creating an organization distinct from NATO for conducting East-West negotiations on contacts, trade, and other non-military aspects of détente.[9] Zbigniew Brzezinski, a member of the Policy Planning Council of the State Department, believed that the uncoordinated paths taken by the Western allies were dangerous to NATO. He recommended a conference of the heads of government in the West to outline plans for multilateral ties with the East to replace many of the bilateral initiatives being undertaken. [10]

Three events in early 1966 dramatized the need for some coordination of the Western détente strategies. First, in March de Gaulle formally ended the French participation in the integrated NATO defense and ordered the Allied Command to remove its headquarters from French soil. With the Americans deeply embroiled in a war in Southeast Asia and the nuclear parity between the super powers throwing into doubt the American nuclear commitment to Europe, de Gaulle insisted that the costs of the defensive coalition had greatly increased while its benefits had declined. The second development in 1966 was the "peace note" sent in March to the East

Europeans by the new "Grand Coalition" government in Bonn. The note offered the West German signature on renunciation of force agreements with the U.S.S.R., Poland, and Czechoslovakia. No mention was of the Oder-Neisse boundary dispute or of recognition for the East German regime and the note was rejected by the Warsaw pact countries. However, the initiative indicated the determination of the F.R.G. leadership to further expand relations with the East, bilaterally if necessary. Finally, also in March, the twenty-third Congress of the C.P.S.U. called for a European security conference excluding the United States. A differentiated approach was again evident as the Soviets sounded conciliatory toward everyone in the West except the Americans and the Germans. They pictured the deepening of détente as a result of "peace forces" in the West and the erosion of American influence in Europe.

The Russians wanted to take advantage of the difficulties in NATO which de Gaulle had brought into sharp focus. They wanted to encourage the "Europe for the Europeans" aspect of de Gaulle's policies and they believed that a security conference excluding the U.S. would be a strong support for that attitude in Western Europe. But de Gaulle was not easily led. In a tour of the Eastern bloc in the spring of 1966 de Gaulle referred to the G.D.R. during a speech in Moscow as "the zone of occupation". Such wording could not have pleased his Russian hosts. France had more in common with the smaller countries of Eastern Europe who resented super power domination and the Soviets were aware of that empathetic situation. They hoped to use French anti-bloc feelings as a lever against the West Germans but at the same time they had to be careful of three possible side effects of such a tactic. First, they did not want anti-German policy to drive the F.R.G. more irrevocably into the arms of the Americans. Secondly, they could not be too conciliatory toward de Gaulle because of his refusal to recognize the G.D.R. To do so might undermine the stability of the Pankow regime. Lastly, the Soviets could not let the French nationalistic rhetoric infect the East Europeans with anti-Russian sentiment.

Intra-bloc problems were also plaguing the Eastern camp. The East Europeans by 1965 had reversed the balance of raw material trade with the U.S.S.R. They were importing raw materials from the Soviet Union and exporting finished goods which created an unfavorable trade balance for the Russians. The increasing economic sophistication of the East European countries increased the attractiveness of Western economic institutions as well as the possibilities for mutually advantageous trade relations with the

West. Yugoslavia's accession to GATT in 1966 was a course which the Soviets feared would be repeated by CEMA member states. The Romanians were becoming particularly independent in their public statements. Although they went along with the general line on the dangers of West German "revanchism" and the calls for dissolution of the blocs, the Romanian emphasis was on the latter in their policy statements on European security.

In the midst of these growing uncertainties within the two opposed camps in Europe the Warsaw Pact issued an appeal in July 1966 for a conference to deal with European security. Issued from Bucharest, the "Declaration on Strengthening Peace and Security in Europe" was an important event in the history of the European security conference. Two main features of previous communications concerned with European security issued by the Warsaw Pact were the need for dissolution of the military alliances and the general ambiguity concerning American participation in any pan-European negotiations. The Bucharest Declaration of 1966 reiterated the appeals for dissolving the blocs. No mention was made however of the web of bilateral treaties connecting the East Europeans to the U.S.S.R. and to each other apart from the Warsaw Treaty Organization. The important change was on the question of the American role in European security arrangements. First, a conference was explicitly called for and the potential for such a meeting for European security was described:

> ....*convocation of a general European conference to discuss the questions of ensuring security in Europe and organizing general European co-operation would be of great positive importance. The agreement reached at the conference could be expressed, for example, in the form of a general declaration on cooperation for the maintenance and strengthening of European security. Such a declaration could provide for an undertaking by the signatories to be guided in their relations by the interest of peace, to settle disputes by peaceful means only, to hold consultations and exchange information on questions of mutual interest, and to contribute to the all-round development pf economic, scientific, technical, and cultural relations. The declaration should be open to all interested states.* [11]

This was one of the earliest of the fairly detailed expectations of what areas a conference might deal with and what it might achieve. The

Declaration from Bucharest went on to clarify who might participate. Acceptable participants would be, along with the states of the Warsaw Pact, "members of the North Atlantic Treaty and neutrals......the Warsaw Treaty States make no exceptions. It is up to each state to choose between participating in the discussion and the solution of European problems or not...". Why did the Russians appear to change their position on U.S. participation? They may simply have realized that the West Europeans would not come to a multilateral conference of the type suggested without American participation. By being ambivalent in the past on the participation issue, the Soviets may have hoped to test Western solidarity. Now that NATO solidarity did seem shaken, but not broken to the extent that the West Europeans were ready to exclude the Americans from European security arrangements, the Russians may have decided that the conference could be used <u>with</u> American participation to dissolve the formal bloc structures which had institutionalized the American presence. They may also have hoped to receive some concession from the West in return for this concession on U.S. participation.

At any rate, the Bucharest Declaration did not change the other Soviet positions on the issues which divided Europe. These included formal recognition by the West of the East German regime, recognition of the Oder-Neisse boundary between Poland and the G.D.R. and the boundary between the two Germanys, renunciation of the Munich Agreement of 1938 as null and void *ab initio*, and rejection of access to nuclear weapons by both Germanys either through internal production or "indirectly through alignments of states...or any form of participation in the control of such weapons." The West was not ready to accept these positions but nevertheless the sentiments of many Western observers were won over by the Declaration and its concession on participation. Partly because there was no change on the substantive issues stances and because the U.S. was preoccupied with Vietnam and the difficulties in NATO, the Bucharest Declaration brought no positive response from the West.

If there were mixed feelings in the West over how to respond to the Bucharest Declaration and concerning Ostpolitik generally, perceptions of the purpose of détente and Westpolitik were also divergent in the East. At one level, the idea of a security conference was a source of agreement among the Eastern allies. However, the conference proposal was only one facet of a larger policy. The ultimate purpose of détente was the real issue. For the G.D.R., recognition as a full-fledged state was the ultimate goal and a multi—lateral conference would aid in that quest, perhaps even achieve it. Romania on the other hand sought more room to maneuver in its relations with the U.S.S.R. and either bilateral or multilateral exchanges with the West, as long as they were out of the bloc context, would lend credence to their independence of action. All of the East Europeans were interested in troop reductions in Central Europe but here Poland in particular actively developed and advocated possible schemes for achieving that end. Another source of general agreement was on the need for international recognition of the legitimacy of the existing boundaries in Central Europe. All the states of the East wanted the West to recognize the division of Germany as permanent as well as the Oder-Neisse boundary between East Germany and Poland. A European security conference could ratify these arrangements "officially". Finally, development of East-West contacts outside the military context as mentioned in the Bucharest Declaration was desired by all the East Europeans. Hungary, Czechoslovakia, and Romania stressed this positive aspect of the proposed conference. Hungary was particularly interested in access to Western technology to aid in regional development and co-operation schemes such as in the Danube River valley. Czechoslovakia felt the pull of Western trade and know-how as it began to reform its economy under the direction of Professor Ota Sik in 1966-1967. Novotny, General Secretary of the Czech Communist Party, grew fearful of the development as it began to challenge the authority of the government, but still both the Czech reformers and Novotny hoped that a conference on European security and cooperation would benefit Czechoslovakia economically as well as help stabilize it politically. Only the conference and its aftermath could prove which of the different perceptions of the effect of the conference would prove to be true.

For the United States, of particular interest was the meaning behind the conciliatory Russian approach heralded by the Bucharest Declaration. Was this conference idea a Trojan horse? Evidence of Soviet pliability started piling up. The U.N. Eighteen Nation Disarmament Committee (ENDC) had been dismissed in the fall of 1965 when the U.S.S.R. insisted that it could not negotiate disarmament while the U.S. waged imperialist war in Southeast Asia. But when the ENDC reconvened in January 1966 the Russians were ready to talk. In May 1966 the Soviets responded to an American initiative to begin negotiations aimed at banning orbiting nuclear devices and precluding sovereign claims over the moon or planets. In September agreement was reached on exchanging weather photos and in November direct commercial flights between the U.S and U.S.S.R. were agreed upon.

There were many speculations as to the Soviet intent behind this spate of agreeability. One possibility was an intense Russian desire to complete a non-proliferation treaty for nuclear weapons (NPT) which would prevent the F.R.G. from gaining access to such weapons. Negotiations on this issue did in fact progress, a draft finally being signed in August, 1967, but the section concerning inspection for verification of compliance was left blank. Nor was West German acceptance of the NPT immediately forthcoming. A second possible reason for Soviet congeniality was the perceived fragmentation of the Soviet alliance system which was becoming as evident as that within the NATO ranks. The Sino-Soviet split seemed particularly relevant to Russian policy towards Europe. Internal tension in the Soviet Union itself over resource allocation and reform of the economic system also may have induced Soviet leaders to seek lower levels of tension in Europe. Soviet investments in the Third World had not panned out as expected and were indeed becoming a drag on the Soviet economies and this too might have led to the renewed emphasis on conciliation rather than confrontation. Lastly, of course there was the nuclear stalemate which itself may have convinced the Soviet leaders of the impossibility of making gains by appearing bellicose. [12]

Along with confusion over Soviet intensions was uncertainty in the West over the best methods for carrying out the policy of détente and over the ultimate aim of that policy. For the Americans détente often seemed to take second place to their concern over the fragmentation of NATO. The U.S. hoped that military security would provide the cohesion for the Western alliance. The Americans emphasized the need for Western solidarity in the face of rapidly growing Russian conventional military capabilities. If the Western Alliance lost its credibility as a viable defense for Western Europe, the Americans and most Europeans argued, Russian military strength could psychologically influence the direction of West European foreign policy and perhaps even their domestic political situations to the advantage of the communists. This line was so important to the United States that it probably hampered efforts at bilateral superpower arrangements in disarmament and other areas as well as making Soviet-West European détente more difficult. American spokesmen stressed the limited nature of détente in Europe. Basic issues remained unresolved they warned. One analyst noted an "American inclination to differentiate between a situation in which conflicts could be kept under control and a situation conducive to the settlement of basic disputes." [13]

Vietnam, the NPT, and Charles de Gaulle all added to the pressures on NATO. Despite American efforts to gain European support for their venture in Asia, the European allies remained cool, even hostile, toward American intervention. The Europeans were loath to become entangled with global commitments, a danger which was further underscored by the Middle East war of 1967. The NPT was a source of resentment for the West Germans and the French because it smacked of superpower condominium especially at a time when nuclear sharing in NATO was by no means settled and when the superpowers continued their own strategic arms race.

Of course, in many ways Charles de Gaulle epitomized the anti-superpower feelings present in both halves of Europe. In both the East and the West de Gaulle was admired for his forthright patriotism but at the same time reality prevented more than ambivalent adherence to his tactics by those who desired more independence of action from superpower influence. That de Gaulle's removal of French forces from NATO was a shock that forced reexamination of the purpose of NATO cannot be denied. But it should not be assumed from those troubles that sentiment in Western Europe generally was anti-NATO. As Robert Hunter commented, NATO's good health had become a pervasive belief.

> (There existed) a public appearance of solidarity and normal functioning, as though NATO were practically another government with a constitution, instead of a collection of more or less sovereign states that subscribed to a treaty.......the NATO code of desirable behavior came to stand for reality, to such a point that the French government's reevaluation of the worth of NATO against its costs - a computation central to the continuation of any treaty arrangement – was greeted by some governments as though it were treason. [14]

In an important speech delivered in October 1966 in the midst of the Soviet "peace offensive" and de Gaulle's shaking NATO, President Johnson outlined the American position on these developments. Three essential points were made, the first two and most important being the need for NATO modernization and strengthening, and secondly the continued American support for further economic and political integration in

Western Europe. Third on the list of priorities was "to quicken progress in East-West relations." There was no heresy about dissolution of the military blocs as in Soviet communiques, rather the blocs were to be maintained to "provide a framework in which West and East can act together in order to assure the security of all." Eventual reunification of Germany was referred to several times, but always as something to be accomplished after East-West reconciliation rather than as a pre-requisite for the conciliation.

President Johnson mentioned both the American desire to conclude a non-proliferation agreement and the desire to form a nuclear planning group for NATO to replace previous schemes concerning nuclear sharing. The group, formally initiated in December 1966, focused on a multilateral approach to solving the problems encountered in planning the American nuclear responsibility rather than on dividing that responsibility in some way. This development in NATO as well as in other areas of defense planning and coordination were described in the NATO communique of December 1966 which also noted the transference of NATO headquarters from Paris to Brussels.

An important aspect of the Johnson speech in October was its admission that the division of Europe could only be healed with the consent of the Eastern European countries and the consent of the Soviet Union. Bridge-building through economic incentives was still the tool for getting that consent, and Johnson listed several economic "concessions" to the East, including guaranteed commercial credits and easing of East-West trade restrictions on non-strategic materials. He hoped that the East would be willing to make political compromises in order to be granted these favors. Actually, American action in this policy of economic liberalization in East-West relations was far behind that of the West Europeans. The trade between West and East Europe exclusive of the U.S.S.R. was over five billion dollars in 1965, while the American trade with those countries was less than two million dollars. [15] Nevertheless, this form of peaceful engagement was an essential thrust of American policy toward the communist bloc despite the moral hesitancy and concern over NATO solidarity. It was an approach essential to acceptance of the conference on security and co-operation in Europe. Z. Brzezinski, one of the principle advocates of peaceful engagement, described its purpose in 1967 this way:

> *I am convinced it would be idle, and probably count-*
> *er-productive to concentrate on stimulating East European*

*nationalism or hostility to the Soviet Union; to be sure the
more independence there is in the East the better – but as
a means and not as an end in itself. Some East European
countries can act as transmission belts by moving ahead
of the Soviet Union, but not for the purpose of separating
themselves entirely from the Soviet Union rather for the
purpose of promoting a different kind of East-West relationship.* [16]

Brzezinski went on to call for a negotiating change within the context
of peaceful engagement which had significance for the proposed European
security conference:

*It seems to me that the time has come to think also beyond
purely bilateral relations. After all, in the final analysis,
bilateralism is purely a technical term for a European
Europe articulated by General de Gaulle. It seems to me
that we have passed the first phase – confrontation; we are
completing the second phase – the exploration of bilateral
relationships; and we are on the eve of a third phase – trying
to build multilaterally an East-West relationship.* [17]

Although this statement could be construed simply as another example
of an American exhorting the West Europeans to maintain bloc solidarity,
its emphasis on multilateralism could also mean less dependence on bilateral superpower conciliation for solving the problems of Europe.

If it seemed to Brzezinski that the second stage of bilateralism was
being completed, it did not seem so to the French. The French were optimistic about their *Ostpolitik* and about its bilateral form. In November
1966 the French Foreign Minister Couve de Murville described French
relations with the East in this way: "From formal, infrequent and negative
they have become numerous, cordial, constructive and all told, normal."
[18] But there were flaws in the French strategy, ironically because the very
independence of action which de Gaulle advocated for nations in both
East and West could mean that those governments might rationally and
freely choose not to aggravate relationships with the superpowers simply
for the chimera of independent action. When de Gaulle visited Poland in
1967, General Secretary Gomulka made clear that Polish foreign policy

was based on maintaining its ties with the U.S.S.R. and the other states of Eastern Europe. On the other side, a trip by Kosygin to London in February 1967 produced little more than some superficial agreements on trade and technical cooperation. The government of Prime Minister Wilson expressed its continuing commitment to NATO, refusing pointedly to repudiate the U.S. role in Vietnam. Part of the reason for the British hardline was found in the British need for support from the F.R.G. in Britain's bid for EEC membership.

The West Germans had come in for more verbal abuse from the Soviets after the Romanians broke rank and established diplomatic relations with West Germany in January 1967. Brezhnev made it clear that recognition of the G.D.R. remained a prerequisite for normalization of the situation in Europe. Although the Romanians went ahead with their independent policy, the new Soviet hardline prevented the on-going talks between the F.R.G. and Czechoslovakia and Hungary from coming to fruition. The Russians could not prevent the Romanians from their opening to the West, but they did try to belittle the diplomatic exchange by pointing out that it was neither important nor a trend toward peace unless the F.R.G. changed its positions on the recognition of the G.D.R., the boundary disputes, etc. The Soviet tendency to down play the effectiveness of détente when speaking to its allies while acting warmly toward the West was rather similar to the American balancing act.

Soviet references to "European security" which in 1966 had been expressed with the hope of eroding American influence in Europe were changing to a more defensive tone in 1967. Moscow had apparently grown uneasy at the lack of control it had over the effects in the East of the *Ostpolitik* being conducted by the Grand Coalition government in Bonn. In March 1967 the Russians signed several new bilateral treaties with the East Europeans. The G.D.R., which until then had a bilateral treaty with the U.S.S.R. only, was incorporated into the bilateral treaty structure which bound the East Europeans together distinctly from the Warsaw Treaty.

A conference of European communist parties held at Karlovy Vary, Czechoslovakia in April 1967 underlined the renewed vigor of Soviet efforts at preventing erosion of their position in Eastern Europe. Notable absences from the conference were Yugoslavia and Romania. The sixteen ruling and non-ruling parties which did attend signed a final communique which was replete with charges of "neo-Nazism" in the F.R.G. and with predictions of the inevitable demise of NATO on its twentieth birthday in 1969 due to

West European resentment at the domination of American capital over their economies. The statement played on anti-American sentiment in Western Europe, concluding with this point: "The European peoples are capable of deciding themselves the questions of peace and security in their continent. Let them take the destinies of Europe in their own hands."

Unquestionably, the Karlovy Vary statement represented a regression from the progress toward a European security conference. The U.S.S.R. toughened its positions on the various issues in dispute compared with the Bucharest Declaration of July 1966. The change was in response to what appeared to the Russians to be an attempt at subverting the Eastern alliance by the new German government. The Karlovy Vary statement claimed that:

> ....*there are no signs the new government of the so-called coalition has abandoned the imperialist goals of its pre-decessors. On the contrary, despite assurances of peaceful designs, it upholds claims to represent all of Germany, continues to strive to swallow up the G.D.R., to restore Germany within the frontiers of 1937, refuses to recognize the unlawfulness of the Munich diktat, continues to advance provocative claims to West Berlin, in striving to get access to nuclear arms.*

The joint statement listed four points which had to be accepted if détente were to deepen in Europe. These were recognition of the European boundaries, particularly the Oder-Neisse line and the boundary between the two Germanys; recognition of the G.D.R.'s sovereignty and renunciation of the F.R.G.'s claim to represent all of Germany; exclusion of any opportunity for the West Germans to gain access to nuclear arms "in any form", either European, multilateral, or Atlantic; and recognition of the 1938 Munich agreement as invalid *ab initio*. The last point was given much more prominence at Karlovy Vary than in the Bucharest Declaration to counteract West German assurances to Czechoslovakia that the Munich treaty was dead. The Soviets wanted to restrain those views in in Czechoslovakia which favored rapprochement with Bonn. [19] Another difference was the absence of any reference at Karlovy Vary to eventual German reunification. The Bucharest Declaration had envisioned a possible reunification process.

Other points in the Karlovy Vary statement included an appeal for a non-proliferation treaty, a call for the liquidation of artificial trade barriers between East and West, and a restatement of Eastern desire to dissolve the military blocs facing each other in Europe. It was suggested that West Berlin become a separate political entity. Although in Brezhnev's address to the conference he did mention that détente had been advanced "largely (as the) result of improvement in bilateral relations between the States of the East and West," the overall emphasis of the conference was on the need for multi-lateral approaches to European security. Multilateralism did not now, however, include the United States. Support was reaffirmed for "a conference of all European states on the question of security and peaceful cooperation in Europe." The appeal was directed to all peace-loving forces (even "the Christian forces, the Catholics and Protestants, the believers of all religious denominations who motivate their striving for peace and social justice by religious convictions") to expand their actions for collective security on "a continental scale." Included in the drive for peace were "bourgeois groupings which display a realistic approach to modern reality and who wish to rid their countries of dependence on the United States and are ready to support the policy of European security."

The anti-American and anti-West German swing from 1966 to 1967 was quite evident. Ironically, it was not prompted by overtly aggressive behavior by those capitalist countries but by what was a more subtle, and therefore more threatening, "subversion by the feather." This Soviet fear was not allayed by Western professions of good intentions. For example, Averell Harriman, U.S. ambassador-at-large, claimed at the same time that the Karlovy Vary conference was in the process of condemning Western "bridge-building" that, "the hope that the peoples of Western and Eastern Europe can work together for the common good and can only be realized if both accept the existence of each other's political systems and avoid interference in each other's internal affairs." [20]

The period from about mid-1966 until the invasion of Czechoslovakia in August 1968 was one of opportunity and some degree of success for Russian policy toward Europe aimed at undermining U.S. credibility in the European power structure. However, the Soviets could only make limited gains from the opportunities arising within NATO due to difficulties within their own bloc. The cautious differentiation of views among the Warsaw Pact allies over the purpose of a conference on European security was one example of the dangers which might have arisen had the Soviets tried to turn the West German Ostpolitik against the United States. Instead, it was necessary to blunt the German initiatives even though it hurt the chances for a truly European solution to the division of the continent. Nevertheless, the Soviet Union continued to use the conciliatory approach toward the less threatening states of Europe and appealed to the "progressive" forces within those states. An example was Podgorny's visit to Finland in May 1967. Warmer relations had developed between Finland and the U.S.S.R. since the Finnish Communist party had been allowed to join the coalition government in the summer of 1996. Podgorny during his visit praised the Finnish support for the European security conference idea. But playing to the minor European powers did not solve the Soviet dilemma. Revealingly, the Karlovy Vary conference was the last to issue a communique in which suggestions for dissolving NATO and the Warsaw pact were given prominence. From mid-1967 on, this idea was deleted from conference proposals. The Eastern bloc was showing enough strain without such provocative projections.

Although the Soviet Union found it expedient to publicly reject the overtures of the Bonn government and reasserted all the old prerequisites for normalization of relations with West Germany, the Russians still tried to discretely demonstrate a willingness to bargain. At subterranean levels the Kiesinger government in Bonn had indicated that it was prepared to reject the Munich Agreement ab initio and Foreign Minister Brandt had been unofficially invited to Prague. [21] While there were reasons why they might not have been too happy with this particular demarche, they did continue to engage the Germans in confidential negotiations. At those non-public discussions the Germans indicated that they were considering bi-lateral renunciation of force agreements with their Eastern neighbors. For their part, the Soviets narrowed their prerequisite list in these quiet talks to recognition of the G.D.R. The F.R.G. was not prepared to go that far.

In December 1967 a report on the future tasks of the NATO alliance, the Harmel report, was issued. Although lacking in concrete suggestions, the statement did mention the desirability of balanced force reduction discussions between the blocs as soon as some of the political issues in Europe were on the road to settlement. This reference to disarmament, mentioned in both the communique from the December NATO meeting in Brussels and the annexed Harmel report, was the Western response to the very unsatisfactory Karlovy Vary communique from the East. Importantly, the rather chilly language of Karlovy Vary was not met in the same fashion by NATO whose message sounded very "co-existential" by comparison. References were made to working together with the countries of the East for European peace and the need for a stable and just order in Europe. Although the idea of a European security conference was not specifically addressed, the Harmel report noted that, "currently the development of contacts between the countries of Western and Eastern Europe is mainly on a bi-lateral basis. Certain subjects, of course, require by their very nature, a multilateral solution."

Détente forces in the West were discouraged by the Soviet response to the December 1967 NATO statement.

> With one voice, Soviet propaganda organs asserted that NATO's 'aggressive nature' remained unchanged despite attempts to put on a 'new face' at Brussels with the adoption of the 'so-called Harmel Plan.' Thus, deriding 'talk about plans to modernize the Atlantic Alliance' so as to make it 'a practical instrument for co-operation with the East', a Moscow commentator declared that 'the Brussels session shows plainly enough that NATO will continue as an instrument of war.' [22]

Despite the criticisms from the Soviet Union, the West continued to advocate détente as the most effective policy for achieving their interests in Europe. What were those interests? The fundamental question was, and continues to be, what priority should Western nations given to stability in Europe in their efforts to normalize inter-bloc relations? Should the status quo be recognized, explicitly, in order to preserve stability, or was the division of Europe inherently unstable anyway? Paradoxically, in the 1950s and early 1960s when both sides found the situation in Europe particularly threatening and unacceptable, the logic of confrontation rigidified the status quo, while from the mid-sixties onward when both sides grew to accept the status quo as a rather stable and acceptable situation, the resulting détente appeared to increase instability in Europe. The logic of détente allowed new sources of instability within the blocs to become stronger. This change was important for the possibility of acceptance of the proposed multi-lateral security conference because it tended to break down the bipolar adversary relationship which would have been incompatible, at least in its highly rigid form, with a conference that would deal with security in Europe outside the bloc format.

The Americans had been the most hesitant in their approaches to the east among the NATO countries. A close second had been the West Germans. With the F.R.G.'s détente offensive undertaken by the Grand Coalition, pressure was increasing on the U.S. to be more flexible in its attitude toward the eastern bloc. Britain's attitudes had been ambiguous toward détente so as not to anger either the French or the Germans and thereby jeopardize their chances for membership in the EEC. But as the West German position changed the U.K. "seemed confident that the European détente would last and they were therefore anxious to use it in order to cut defense expenditures, to make the military environment more secure, and thus to make the climactic preconditions for an eventual political settlement." [23] During his February 1967 trip to London, Soviet Premier Kosygin had tried to get English backing for the Russian security conference idea but ambiguity on U.S. participation prevented any agreement. However, when British Prime Minister Wilson visited Moscow in January 1968 the joint communique issued at the end of the discussions stated that a security conference "could be valuable, subject to the necessary preparation." [24] Further indication of change in the British opinion was provided by a motion submitted by fifty Labor MPs in June 1968 calling on Prime Minister Wilson to improve relations with the G.D.R. [25]

Along with pressure from the large West European powers for a more favorable attitude toward a European security conference, the smaller countries were also advocating a multi-lateral meeting between East and West. In February 1968 a Dutch parliamentary discussion concluded that greater efforts toward convening a conference were necessary. A month later Austrian Foreign Minister Kurt Waldheim visited Moscow and agreed in principle to a security conference but he balked at exclusion of the United States. [26] Italy took a similar position.

Among the Western allies, the French were the most unequivocal in their support for a European security conference. De Gaulle's "Europe from the Atlantic to the Urals" at times seemed to signify a new Franco-Soviet arrangement to replace Soviet-American hegemony. Even more likely, however, was that De Gaulle desired to undermine the influence of both superpowers in Europe. General De Gaulle visited Poland in September 1967 and he travelled to Romania in May 1968 preaching his middle-way. But events at home caught up with him while he was in Romania. Student riots spread to the workers, France was paralyzed, and De Gaulle rushed home. Caught in a predicament, the General blamed the rioting on "communists" and his relations with the U.S.S.R. were badly damaged. Thereafter,

Gaullist obstruction would be less threatening to Atlantic unity although its impact had brought a new perspective to all Europeans. Now, while the West Europeans conducted policy toward the Soviet Union in primarily non-military terms, tension within the NATO alliance came from the American focus on its global strategic relationship with the U.S.S.R. and on the trauma of the Vietnam War.

With the Soviet security conference proposal gaining momentum, the NATO Ministerial Council made a move to regain the initiative. At the NATO Foreign Ministers meeting at Reykjavik in June 1967 the participants, with the exception of France, issued a proposal for mutual and balanced force reductions between the blocs. While stating in the beginning of the communique their continued non-recognition of the G.D.R. and their resolve to overcome any harassment of the access routes to Berlin (which had been recently hampered by the G.D.R.) the NATO Ministers sought to counter the Soviet conference proposal with their own proposal for specifically military negotiations on a bloc-to-bloc basis (a basis which France rejected). No mention was made in the communique of a possible European security conference. The statement issued announced that the

> ....Ministers agreed that it was desirable that a process leading to mutual force reductions should be initiated. To that end they decided to make all necessary preparations for discussions of this subject with the Soviet Union and other countries of Eastern Europe as they call on them to join in this search for progress towards peace.

This "Reykjavik signal" was important in the progress towards the eventual European security conference because, although not stated explicitly, negotiations between the blocs on mutual force reductions would thereafter be the Western quid pro quo for accepting the conference proposal. The West had met the concept of a security conference, which might only ratify the status quo, benefit the U.S.S.R. economically, and conjure an atmosphere of unreal détente, with a demand for real, tangible changes, i.e. troop reductions in central Europe. As the West officially chose to ignore the proposal for a security conference, so the Soviets ignored this Western proposal for troop reduction talks and they continued to advocate repeatedly in their public statements the conference idea.

While progress toward the conference was slowed primarily by the intransigence of the superpowers, another multi-lateral treaty, even broader in scope, was finally signed after more than two years of consideration. This was the Nuclear Non-Proliferation Treaty. Signed on July 1, 1968, after being jointly submitted to the United Nations by the U.S. and U.S.S.R. in March, the treaty originally included sixty-one countries. There were important holdouts. Two of the five countries known to possess nuclear weapons, China and France, refused to sign. Half of the thirty-four nations of the world who possessed nuclear reactors did not sign. Some of the important initial holdouts were India, Israel, the F.R.G., Japan, and Canada. Despite these limitations, the treaty did demonstrate something important, a fact that has implications for the policy of détente and for the eventual convening of the European security conference. Despite their many differences in ideology and opposed national interests, the superpowers can find bases of shared interest and they can convert those shared interests into concrete programs. The Soviets might have hoped to embarrass the Americans by the treaty which was resented by some West Europeans because it smacked of superpower condominium. They might also have hoped that the NPT would slow China's nuclear growth and that it would prevent West Germany from gaining access to nuclear weapons. But since neither of these countries would sign the treaty, this could not have been the only Soviet motivation for supporting the NPT. We must accept the fact that the superpowers both agreed on the need to control the destabilizing effects of nuclear proliferation, a destabilization which could threaten their relatively secure balance of strategic military power.

The Soviet Union, already nervous over the signs of nationalist independence within their bloc watched carefully the development of liberal programs within the Dubcek government of Czechoslovakia. Dubchek, having come to power through election by the Czech Central Committee Plenum in January, 1968, deposing the fifteen-year-old Novotny regime, had begun to introduce social and economic policies aimed at relaxing some of the restraints of communist orthodoxy. Symbolic of their desire for independence from the Russians, the Dubcek government signed a treaty of friendship with Romania, the most outspoken advocate of East European independence. The treaty not only limited the purpose of the Warsaw Pact to action against NATO, but it also lacked any explicit reference to "the West German threat". [27] This treaty was signed on August 16, 1968; four days before Warsaw Pact troops occupied Prague.

I will not go into detail on the events leading to the invasion of

Czechoslovakia. The Soviets had weathered the "Polish Spring" a few months earlier. Gomulka, First Secretary of the Polish Communist Party, had been able to maintain internal Party control and Soviet troops were not needed. The Russians demonstrated considerable ambivalence to the situation in Czechoslovakia. The Politburo of the C.P.S.U. was apparently split on what action to take, or not to take. In fact, it looked as though the crisis had passed when lightning struck, and the attack was lightning swift in its military precision. The troops in the invasion, though from all the bloc countries except Romania, were placed directly under the direction of the Soviet high command rather than the Warsaw Pact structure.

Though militarily flawless, politically the invasion could only be justified if there had been a very immediate threat to Soviet Security. Otherwise, the whole situation proved extremely embarrassing, and damaging, to the Soviet world image. The Russians, after grasping the Czech government by the throat, could find no Czech voice to say, "Yes, we asked the Pact forces into Prague to prevent Western subversion," as the Soviets claimed was the case. Dubcek and other Czech leaders were forcibly taken to Moscow. The gross violation of Czech sovereignty was condemned even by the Chinese who were in the seemingly contradictory position of condemning the Soviet invasion even though Dubcek's reforms were diametrically opposed to the Chinese view of communist Orthodoxy. While the East European countries generally kept a discreet silence, other communist parties all over the world expressed their condemnation of the Soviet move. Even those attempts to separate themselves from the Russian action did not prevent a serious loss of credibility in the eyes of their own populations. Most importantly for the security conference proposal, the invasion brought into sharp focus the difference between Eastern and Western understandings of what détente in Europe meant. Perhaps Western observers had perceived more symmetry between the bloc structures than really existed. They did not therefore conceive that the fragmentation which was affecting both blocs would be met by blunt military force in the East. At any rate, the subsequent "Brezhnev Doctrine" concerning the "limited sovereignty of socialist states" within the "socialist commonwealth" prompted deep rethinking of the methods and purposes of the West's détente policies.

The NATO Foreign Ministers meeting scheduled for December, 1968 was moved up to mid-November to discuss the situation created by the Czech invasion. The meeting, in condemning the invasion, emphasized the renewed proof of the need for Western solidarity and called for stronger defense, greater military expenditures, and better coordination of military strategy among the NATO countries. The ministers rejected the notion of a "socialist commonwealth". Nevertheless, the communique issued by NATO Foreign Ministers, while noting that the invasion had dealt a serious blow to the possibility of MBFR talks and that it had damaged détente generally, still affirmed that the NATO countries would continue to base their policies on a search for relaxing tensions between the blocs. The basic problem for the West was clear:

> *If the West were to swallow Czechoslovakia's subjugation with little more than a gulp of moral indignation and offer to go back to business as usual, the policy of the Soviet hard-liners would be validated and the position of the moderates further undermined. If, on the other hand, the West refused to treat the situation as a mere "family affair" within the Warsaw camp and put some sting into its disapproval, the Soviet hard-liners could be expected to claim that they were right all along about meddling interference from the West, while the moderates would find themselves either obliged to agree or placed in the compromising position of siding with the meddlesome adversary. In short, the currency of the moderation in East-West diplomacy seemed to have been debased by the Soviet handling of the Czechoslovak situation.* [28]

The Soviets also found themselves wrestling with the conundrum of how to advance prospects for influence in Western Europe while preventing erosion of their hegemony in the East. The invasion of Czechoslovakia was aimed at solving the problem. The Russian leaders finally decided to act decisively in the East to set the precedent of willingness to use force and then they could only wait to see if "peaceful coexistence" could be reinstituted with the West. If it could be, the East Europeans would be much less likely to let the détente "go to their heads". Thus the Soviet sword fell on their Gordian knot.

The Soviets, having broken out of the rigidity which increasingly had limited their options in foreign policy due to their preoccupation with subversion of the East Europeans by the West's *Ostpolitik*, could now return to their interrupted "peace offensive". The NATO response militarily to the invasion was only symbolic. NATO had been careful during the invasion not to give any indication that intervention was contemplated lest the Soviets react violently and engulf all of Europe, and perhaps the world, in war. Soviet unpredictability had been admirably demonstrated, perhaps a plus for them politically, perhaps not. Even the NATO force increases announced at the November Ministerial meeting were really symbolic, not strategically important. What the NATO countries instead realized was that there was a need to take political steps to make détente in Europe possible once again. They decided that this would entail at least temporary curtailments of most East-West intercourse in order to demonstrate that the price of détente would be Soviet restraint in the Eastern half of Europe. [29]

The invasion of Czechoslovakia undoubtedly did stimulate some increase in cohesion among the NATO allies. Although de Gaulle claimed that the Soviet actin would only be a temporary setback to his independent policy, it was clear that the policy had lost much of its credibility. This contributed to his resignation from office in April, 1969. Speculation about the dissolution of NATO on its twentieth birthday in 1969 was stifled. Despite the reinforced congruence of threat perception for the Atlantic Alliance, NATO still was not given any great sense of ultimate direction and internal differences of opinion remained, submerged, to resurface later when the shock of August, 1968 had worn off.

In East-West relations there was immediately a long list of cancellations of inter-bloc contacts:

> *At the official level...Denmark and Norway called off the visit of Todor Zhivkov, the Bulgarian communist leader, Denmark also canceled the trip of Hungary's Foreign Minister Janos Peter, and France postponed the visit of Wladyslaw Gomulka. Austria declined the visit of the Soviet Foreign Trade Minister, the Hungarian Premier, Janos Fock, and Zhivkov. Michael Stewart, the British Foreign Secretary called off his visits to Bulgaria and Hungary. West Germany postponed the meeting of her Minister of Economic Affairs, Karl Schiller, with his East European counterpart, Horst Scelle. Negotiations between Belgium and Poland on cultural agreement were postponed. A Danish-Poland conference at the ministerial level on problems of disarmament was called off and the Danish Foreign Minister cancelled his visit to the Soviet Union.*

At the unofficial level, as well, a great number of visits were cancelled: the trips to Russia of the Danish Federal Youth Council, the Italian Christian Worker Association, the Oslo Municipal Philharmonic Orchestra, the Swedish Confederation of Trade Unions, the performances of the Bologna Community Theater in Budapest and East Berlin; the visit of a Dutch Parliamentary delegation to Poland; and of the Greater London Council and the Swiss Chamber of Commerce to the Soviet Union. Great Britain cancelled the tour of the Red Army Choir and the Anglo-Soviet historical exhibition in Moscow. The council of the international film festival at Cork, Ireland, did not permit Soviet participation. The performances of the Russian ballet in La Scala were postponed. At some international conferences, the representatives of the five members of the Warsaw Pact were not admitted, at others they walked out after the invasion had been condemned. [30]

Was the Cold War back on? Well, not exactly. The West was trying to send a signal, as strong a signal as possible, without stopping détente. There were no trip cancellations in December 1968 or in January 1969. By January the volume of East-West contacts was back at its pre-invasion level. [31] Both NATO and the Warsaw Pact were soon once again affirming their commitment to establishing a "durable European peace order". The relaxation during 1966 and 1967 had been replaced by growing Soviet anxiety over erosion of its control in Eastern Europe and this was made manifest by the hard line expressed in the Karlovy Vary statement. The invasion of Czechoslovakia capped the steady chilling of East-West relations throughout 1968.

What was the long term effect of the invasion, particularly in light of Soviet desires for a European security conference? There can be little doubt that it certainly delayed the eventual convening of the conference. But if we return to the idea that both sides need to be certain of the security of what they perceive to be their individual vital interests, Western restraint in its reactions served to assure the Soviets that their interests in Eastern Europe were recognized. At the same time NATO made it clear that Soviet repression would increase Western wariness and inhibit mutually beneficial détente. Michael Howard stated concisely the foundation of Western policy and perhaps it is the definition of the relationship of détente policy, both East and West, to "crises" in the international system. He commented that, "Peace does not consist in the absence of international problems; rather it lies in a general willingness to accept such problems, take them not too tragically, and to rely on time and goodwill to soften their sharp edges even if not to solve them." [32] Even though the "mourning period" of the West was callously short by the standards of the more idealistic observers, the invasion of Czechoslovakia remained, and continues to exist like a "ghost at a banquet" in East-West negotiations. This was the price the Soviet Union paid for guaranteeing its position in Eastern Europe.

Western indications of willingness to continue within the "logic of détente" despite the "illogical" Soviet repression were immediately picked up on by the Russians. The harsh Soviet line toward the West Germans, which reached its height by blaming threats from "revanchist Germany" for the Russian intervention in Czechoslovakia, began to be tempered in late 1968. By January 1969 talks were underway between the Soviet Union and West Germany on the possibility of reopening discussions which were aimed at renunciation of force agreements. A headline in the New York Times of January 11, 1969 read, "Bonn and Moscow Seek Closer Ties", and on February 2nd the headline appeared, "Moscow Offers Generosity if Bonn Signs Nuclear Pact". But the Atlantic Alliance, which was seeking détente after the invasion of Czechoslovakia, was different from the alliance which conducted negotiations with the East before that critical event. There was no longer any question of the Soviet Union being a "paper tiger". Few voices called for withdrawing American troops or for loosening the NATO structure. To underline the new emphasis on caution and commitment, a freshly sworn-in American President, Richard Nixon, visited West Berlin in February, 1969.

Perhaps because they felt that their show of force in Czechoslovakia had demonstrated their ability to control any détente between the F.R.G. and the East Europeans, or possibly because the Soviets felt that some concessions were necessary to overcome the "bad press" resulting from their intervention, the Warsaw Pact issued the Budapest Appeal of March, 1969. Up until this time the Russians had held in reserve the card of openly including the F.R.G. in the process of détente, preferring instead to use "neo-Nazism" and "revanchism" in the F.R.G. as a scarecrow for European Unity. The card played in the Budapest Appeal was signed by the Warsaw Pact members at a consultative meeting held in Budapest for sixty communist parties throughout the world. Perhaps another reason for this important change in Soviet tactics was indicated by the participation at the consultative meeting itself, from which six of the fourteen ruling communist parties in the world absented themselves. These were China, Cuba, Albania, Yugoslavia, North Korea, and North Vietnam. It may be that the Soviet Union was more concerned with the reactions of these nations, rather than the nations of the West, to the invasion of Czechoslovakia.

For whomever the expressions of good intent in the Appeal were meant, the document did mark a very important step toward the eventual convening of the Conference on Security and Cooperation in Europe. Most of the vituperative language of the recent past was dropped. There was no longer any talk of dissolving NATO and the Warsaw Pact. Although solving problems in Europe was still predicated on the West's willingness to negotiate with "due regard to existing realities", the recognition of those "realities" was no longer a <u>prerequisite</u> for a security conference. The appeal declared:

> *One of the basic preconditions for safeguarding the security of Europe is the inviolability of the existing European frontiers, including the Oder-Neisse frontiers and those between the German Democratic Republic and the Federal Republic of Germany, recognition of the existence of those two countries, renunciation by the latter of its claims to represent the whole of the German people, and renunciation of possession in any form of nuclear weapons. West Berlin has a special status and does not belong to West Germany.*

But these preconditions were not to hold up the preparations for a conference, as the next paragraph in the statement pointed out:

> *A practical step towards strengthening European security would be a meeting in the immediate future between representatives of all the European states concerned in order to establish by mutual agreement items on its agenda. We are prepared to consider at the same time any other proposal regarding the method for preparing and convening the Conference.*

Although the G.D.R. and Poland got their particular concerns listed specifically, those points were no longer to stand in the way of a multilateral

European security conference. Since at the time the Appeal was issued the Russians were already seriously negotiating with the West Germans bilaterally over a non-aggression pact, they may have hoped that incorporation and recognition of the "preconditions" in an F.R.G. – U.S.S.R. treaty would prevent the other West Europeans from challenging them effectively at the proposed security conference.[33] To make clear that it was the Soviets managing the new line, Ulbricht, the hardline leader of the G.D.R., was invited to Moscow after the Appeal was issued. After his return the East German Politburo issued a declaration stating that the proposed conference should not be based on prerequisites to be fulfilled by either German state.[34]

There was one problem with the Budapest Appeal. Once again, the U.S. and Canada were implicitly excluded from participation in the security conference for Europe. References to participants included "all interested European states." This was one important reason for the very cool response by NATO to the Soviet initiative in its Twentieth Anniversary communique of April, 1969. Obliquely, the NATO Ministers took note of the Soviet proposal:

> *The Allies propose, while remaining in close consultation, to explore with the Soviet Union and the other countries of Eastern Europe which concrete issues best lend themselves to fruitful negotiation and an early resolution. Consequently, they instructed the council to draft a list of these issues and to study how a useful process of negotiation could best be initiated.*

No mention was made of specific Soviet "preconditions for security" nor of a security conference. But the communique did note that in any negotiations, "all governments whose participation would be necessary to achieve a political settlement in Europe should take part", meaning of course the United States and Canada. The NATO Foreign Ministers also included paragraphs calling for respect of sovereignty among the European States, non-interference in the internal affairs of other states, etc., all cited as criticism of the U.S.S.R.'s role in Eastern Europe. The invasion of Czechoslovakia was explicitly remembered. If there were any NATO Ministers who favored a warmer response to the Budapest Appeal they were silenced by a particularly violent anti-NATO statement issued by the official Soviet news agency TASS. The statement was timed to hit the NATO ministerial meeting just as the proposed security conference was coming up for discussion. "This cold war blast, preceded by major Russian naval maneuvers in the Atlantic, soon froze the slightly warmer air which had moved in from Budapest, causing more than one observer to wonder whether that endeavor had not been primarily designed as a distraction from the 1968 invasion of Czechoslovakia." [35]

The U.S.S.R. was pleased by the neutral sponsorship of the conference in the form of a Finnish memorandum sent to all the European states and the U.S. and Canada in May 1969. The note called for a conference to be convened in early 1970. The Soviet Union hoped that pressure by such neutral countries might embarrass the other states of Europe, and if necessary the North Americans too, into coming into the conference. Taking the path of conciliation in Europe was increasingly important for the Soviet Union as the Chinese threat appeared to be growing more serious. Earlier, in March of 1969, before the Budapest Appeal was issued, Chinese and Russian troops battled on the Ussuri River which divides the two countries. The ambivalent, almost schizophrenic nature of Soviet détente policy demonstrated by the TASS "cold war blast" was also apparent in Russian statements about the West to Communist listeners. While appealing for a security conference on the one hand and sounding very reasonable in the process, the Soviets continued to paint the West in the blackest terms before East European and Soviet audiences. Internal vigilance remained strong after 1968 for the Soviet Union despite the gradual return to relaxation in policy toward the West.

Several events in the last six months of 1969 marked that year as perhaps the most crucial in the birth of the Conference on Security and Cooperation in Europe. On the negative side was the demise of the Group of Ten. This Group was organized according to a United Nations General Assembly resolution in 1965 to discuss and possibly forward solutions to the political problems of the divided continent. The members of the Group were Austria, Belgium, Bulgaria, Denmark, Finland, Hungary, Romania, Sweden, and Yugoslavia. The states were joined in 1967 by the Netherlands. Little of importance ever came from their discussions. After attempts at reconciliation in the wake of the invasion of Czechoslovakia the Group's activities ended. [36]

Another negative factor in the process leading toward the security conference was the introduction in June, and repeated thereafter through 1970, of the "People's Congresses" idea. The concept, developed by the U.S.S.R., was to have individuals and selected organizations from all over

Europe attend a conference. According to the June, 1969 Conference of Communist and Workers' Parties in Moscow, "The organization of a broad congress of European peoples, which would prepare for, and facilitate, the holding of a conference of states, is the most important of all these peace initiatives." [37] Perhaps the Soviets felt that such a conference of selected participants would be more sympathetic and controllable than a conference of states. Perhaps they were simply frustrated by Western opposition to the conference. Whatever the reasoning behind the idea, the West perceived the suggestion as a further indication that the Soviets only desired a propaganda platform and also that they still intended to exclude North American participation in European security arrangements if they could.

Despite these unfavorable developments in 1969, other events counterbalanced them enough that late 1969 might be considered the point at which acceptance of the security conference idea really began to snowball. The crucial factor was the October election in West Germany which brought the Social Democratic Party into sole power for the first time. In his first speech on foreign policy, the new Chancellor Willy Brandt declared his intent to normalize relations with the East Europeans – including the G.D.R. Two days later a meeting of the Warsaw Pact in Prague proposed the first specific agenda items for the envisioned security conference. According to the communique these were:

> *(1) The ensuring of European security and renunciation of the use of force in the mutual relations among states in Europe; (2) Expansion of trade, economic, scientific and technical relations on the principle of equal rights aimed at the development of political co-operation among the European states.*

Thus with Brandt publicly recognizing the East German state, the October Warsaw Pact communique was an important counter initiative. It conceded the Western emphasis on the need for painstaking preparation of any eventual conference and "bloc dissolution" talk was entirely absent. Even the range of participation for the conference appeared to be negotiable. The statement said:

> *The Ministers of Foreign Affairs express on behalf of their governments the conviction that in spite of certain still*

unresolved difficulties all issues pertaining to the prepara-
tion and holding of the All-European conference whether
they concern agenda, range of participation or manner of
convening the conference might be settled provided goodwill
and sincere endeavor to achieve mutual understanding are
shown.

Brandt continued to clear the path to the conference by signing in late November, 1969 the Nuclear Non-Proliferation Treaty ("NPT"). Japan followed suit. During the same month the U.S. and U.S.S.R. ratified the NPT. They had already begun the important Strategic Arms Limitation Talks ("SALT") at Helsinki earlier in 1969 at least partly as an attempt to offset the criticisms of superpower nuclear condominium which the NPT had stirred up. Although the European security conference proposal received little attention at a summit meeting of Communist Party and state leaders in Moscow in December, 1969 the attention focused on the bilateral developments between the F.R.G. and Eastern Europe were truly essential to the conference idea. Pleased with Brandt's signature on the NPT, the Soviets at the December meeting put formal recognition of the G.D.R. in the "desirable" category rather than as "precondition" for discussion on a renunciation of force treaty. [38] Later in the month the bilateral negotiations began despite Ulbricht's objections. The Soviets were wary, as their public statements indicated, but they were eager.

Citing as a positive feature the Federal Republic's signing of
the Nuclear Non-Proliferation Treaty and noting the growth
of tendencies in the direction of "realism", the participants
nonetheless expressed the "unanimous view" that sober
vigilance was required in the face of "unceasing dangerous
manifestations" of revanchism and neo-Nazism in West
Germany. This – along with the emphasis on the need for
all states to "establish equal relations with the G.D.R. on
the basis of international law, and to recognize the finality
of existing borders – indicates that the summit conference
was devoted primarily to consultations on the response
to be taken to the initiatives of Ostpolitik. Indeed, within
the month the Soviet and Polish governments announced
that they had undertaken negotiations with Bonn, and the

G.D.R. proposed a treaty between the two German states recognizing their separate existence under international law. These bilateral dealings and their ramifications were to preoccupy the states involved for months to come.[39]

Meanwhile, the West was warming to the "proposal-counter proposal" bargaining over the security conference idea. In December, 1969 the British proposed a Standing Commission on East-West European Relations. ("SCEWER"). They suggested that this might be an alternative to a conference, or a preparatory mechanism for a conference, or a permanent follow-up institution to a conference. It was to be composed of neutral, nonaligned states as well as states from both military blocs. Prime Minister Wilson, describing the proposal, said it envisioned "permanent machinery for dealing with all the problems in Europe that we could solve, economic as well as political and military and the rest."[40]

The British Labour government had been a long-time supporter of the policy of détente, and of the security conference idea. Some Labour leaders had expressed themselves in favor of recognizing the G.D.R. as early as 1960. But the British had followed the German lead in most of its official policy statements. The return of the Conservative Party to power in June, 1970 brought a more cautious approach back to British strategy, more in line with the general NATO line.

The NATO response to the Eastern initiatives confirmed in December, 1969 was expressed at its December ministerial meeting which occurred almost simultaneously with the Communist summit meeting. NATO's position might be characterized as a cautious side-step and counter punch. Major emphasis in the statement issued from the meeting went to the need for MBFR. Thus, repeating the "Reykjavik signal", the Western allies laid the groundwork for their own "precondition" to the security conference proposal. The West also hinted at its future preference on agenda items by expanding the East's call for economic, commercial, scientific, technological, and cultural contacts to "freer movement of people, ideas, and information between the countries of the East and West."

The Ministers praised the bilateral efforts of the F.R.G. and its Ostpolitik. In connection with the security conference proposal, NATO noted the need for progress in these discussions undertaken by the F.R.G. and also for progress in the Four Power Berlin Talks. Four Power Talks had been in existence in the form of an exchange of notes since July, 1969 when the U.S.S.R. announced its readiness to exchange views on the subject with its wartime allies. The Soviet decision was in response to a NATO preconference meeting between the U.S., Britain, France, and West Germany in April, 1969 at which then Foreign Minister Brandt urged the Western allies to engage the U.S.S.R. in talks aimed at improving the Berlin situation.[41] Discussion between ambassadors of the former allies finally began on March 26, 1970 in the former Allied Control building in Berlin. "This building had not witnessed any four-power meetings since the Soviet military governor, Sokolovsky, had put an abrupt end to quadripartite administration of Germany by leaving the Control Council chamber on March 20, 1948".[42] In their December communique the NATO Ministers noted that, "The elimination of difficulties created in the past with respect to Berlin especially with regard to access, would increase the prospects for serious discussions on the other concrete issues which continue to divide East and West."

MBFR received similar mention as perhaps a preliminary to a conference along with the F.R.G.'s bilateral talks and the Berlin discussions. The NATO Ministers did establish MBFR negotiations as a *sine qua non* for a security conference, but they did not accede to the conference proposal either. There was quiet but growing pressure from some of the smaller West European states such as Belgium, Denmark, Norway, and Italy in favor of the conference. But the cautious December statement stressed that NATO intended to "ensure any such meeting should not serve to ratify the present division of Europe" and that there was "as yet, no common interpretation between the East and West on the principles of sovereign equality, political independence, and the territorial integrity of each European state." These principles were considered essential by NATO for peace and security in Europe and the Brezhnev Doctrine seemed to contradict these basic prerequisites.

The American component of NATO hesitancy was underlined by Secretary of State Rogers in an address to the Belgo-American Association at Brussels on December 6, 1970. Warning that negotiations with the Eastern bloc should not lull the West "into a false sense of détente", Rogers described the Soviet security proposal as "based on what appears to be a nebulous and imprecise agenda". Rogers noted areas in which the NATO countries wished action but had been met by Soviet obstinacy. These were in regard to Berlin and MBFR. Success of the F.R.G.'s Ostpolitik was also mentioned as a NATO desideratum. Does the Soviet Union "seek to ratify the existing division of Europe?" Rogers asked. "Does it intend to draw a veil over its subjugation of Czechoslovakia? Does it wish to use a conference to strengthen its control over the trade policies of the other members of the Warsaw Pact?" Warming to his topic, Rogers condemned the entire substance of the Soviet proposal:

> *What is proposed cannot properly be described as a security conference at all. The Warsaw Pact countries have suggested merely (1) that a conference discuss an East-West agreement on the principle of non-use of force – which has been a basic principle of the United Nations Charter for over 20 years, so that another pronouncement of the non-use of force would have no meaning – and (2) increased trade and technical exchanges for which regular diplomatic channels are always available.*

Rogers made clear perhaps the most pressing concern in NATO saying that, "we will not participate in a conference which has the effect of ratifying or acquiescing in the Brezhnev Doctrine."

As if this slap in the face were not sufficient, Rogers concluded his remarks with this jab:

> *The problem that we have relates to our desire to reduce our presence abroad. We have no interest in domination. Wherever we have indicated a desire to reduce our presence, the people affected have indicated that they want us to stay. The problem of the Soviet Union is just the reverse – they want to stay in areas where the people affected clearly would prefer that they not stay.*

Despite these unfriendly comments, the U.S.S.R. persisted in appearing as congenial as possible, at least in the sphere of conference preconditions and preparations. In January 1970 at a press conference in the Soviet Foreign Ministry the Soviets claimed that their ambassador Dobrynin had assured NATO governments prior to their Brussels meeting that the issue of U.S. participation had been decided favorably.[43] The Soviet Union was clearing away obstacles to the conference as rapidly and yet as carefully as it could.

It may be good at this point to look behind some of the events in the period from 1966 and the Bucharest Declaration to the Budapest Appeal of March 1969 and the subsequent rush of "communique diplomacy" which seemed, despite NATO and particularly American hesitancy, to be leading to preparation of a European security conference.

The Soviet Union's proposals from 1966 through 1969, though there were differences among them in tenor and wording occasionally, were generally rather sweeping in their expectations and showed little flexibility on issues such as recognition of the G.D.R., boundaries, and American participation. Usually included in their statements were what appeared through Western eyes to be divisive and propagandistic appeals for dissolution of NATO and the Warsaw Pact. A neo-Stalinist trend seemed to be reasserting itself in the Soviet Union's domestic policies as well as its policy toward the East Europeans during this period and it was reflected to some extent in foreign policy. The invasion of Czechoslovakia, as damaging to the Russian image as Vietnam was to the American's, was the capstone of this definite chilling of détente. Undoubtedly expansion of the war in Vietnam added to this atmosphere change. Despite this, by the end of 1969 the conference proposal had evolved into "a modest scheme significantly influenced by the West."[44] Internal changes in West Germany which enabled Willy Brandt to step up his Ostpolitik in late 1969 were crucial in the regeneration of détente and for the viability of the conference proposal. By February 1970 the Soviet Union could claim that twenty-four European states had expressed themselves in favor of the conference.[45]

Styles of leadership were important factors in the logic of détente that was both damaged and strengthened by the invasion of Czechoslovakia. Brezhnev, by sanctioning the invasion of Czechoslovakia, was demonstrating the Soviet determination to prevent any radical changes in the status quo of Eastern European – Soviet relations. Unlike Khrushchev, Brezhnev was not attacking at the same time the status quo of world "spheres of influence", at least not with broadside tactics.[46] De Gaulle and Brandt were similar to the communist leaders in their disparate views on détente tactics. Brezhnev and Brandt realized that the status quo could only be changed by first accepting it, while Khrushchev and de Gaulle attacked it frontally.[47]

One reason often given for the change in Soviet tactics from vituperation to cajolery was the rise of the Chinese threat. The clash in 1969 on the Ussuri River marked a new low in the volatile contacts between the two communist giants. It was later rumored that the Soviets may even have contemplated a preventive strike against the emerging Chinese nuclear capabilities. As the story goes, they checked this idea out with the Americans who expressed their extreme displeasure with the scheme. One analyst saw this as part of a clever Russian game aimed at allaying Western fears of Russian strength.

> It is nevertheless advantageous for the U.S.S.R. to convince the West that its moves to improve relations are motivated by fears of China. By stressing the China factor, Moscow reduces Western apprehension that détente is being sought for offensive, tactical purposes. Alternatively, an emphasis on the China threat allowed Moscow to reduce the impression that it is seeking agreements out of a sense of economic weakness. This seems to be the real meaning of the officially inspired rumors in Moscow late in 1969, according to which the U.S.S.R. was considering a pre-emptive first strike against Chinese nuclear facilities. By telling Washington what it wanted to hear about the state of Sino-Soviet relations as SALT I began, Moscow was able to communicate an interest in agreement at no cost to its bargaining position.[48]

China condemned the idea of a conference on European security as simply another exercise of superpower condominium in Europe.

A second reason perceived in the West as ulterior to the Soviet desire for a conference was the Russian belief that NATO cohesiveness was breaking down. In fact, the failure of the West to act in unison on the Soviet proposal from Budapest in 1969 had enabled the U.S.S.R. to negotiate directly with the F.R.G. to legitimize Eastern boundaries. The West was adamant about U.S. participation in any multilateral conference, but a Soviet concession on that point did not really enhance Western solidarity. Many in the West believed that implicit in the idea of a conference on security in Europe, despite the disappearance of calls for dissolving the military blocs, was the possibility that a system of security for all of Europe, however tenuous, might further undermine the raison d'être of NATO. Others felt that the conference's stress on pan-Europeanism might hinder progress of the European Community toward political union. Without a similar web of bilateral treaties as exists in the East, the Western Alliance might succumb to fissiparous pressures. Thus the Soviets were in favor of bilateral East-West contacts, such as the F.R.G.- Poland talks which began in February 1970 and the historic beginning of talks between the two Germanys in March 1970, as well as advocating the multilateral conference idea.

A third possible motive behind the Soviet eagerness for a conference was believed to be a search for international recognition of the Soviet hegemony in Eastern Europe. Like the "China factor", this would be a defensive rationale, an attempt to preserve what the U.S.S.R. already controls. This argument portrays divisive tendencies in the Soviet bloc as much more serious than those in the Western Alliance. The "certainty" which developed due to strategic parity between the military blocs and that formed the basis for détente between the alliances was a threat to the cohesion of the "socialist commonwealth". If a security conference would ratify the Brezhnev Doctrine, the Soviet Union might more easily continue to control by force the pressures for diversity and national autonomy in Eastern Europe. The desire for technical contacts, trade developments, and extended influence in Western Europe, all believed to be important to Soviet foreign policy, is in conflict to some degree with the Russian fear that its grip may be slipping in Eastern Europe. When the invasion of Czechoslovakia made it clear that the Soviets would risk the economic and political gains of détente to maintain the status quo in Eastern Europe they were in fact setting a precondition for the security conference. The West would have to accept the right of the U.S.S.R. to act with military force to insure the integrity of the "socialist commonwealth". At least many in the West believed this was the connection, although many East Europeans believed just the reverse.

The West accepted this precondition despite official protestations to the contrary. Brandt's Ostpolitik was based on a longer range hope that, once the U.S.S.R. felt confident of its influence in Eastern Europe, then the inter-bloc relationships might become more fluid to the benefit of both halves of Europe economically and in terms of autonomy from the superpowers. Questions of ideological conflict and the Soviet meaning of "peaceful coexistence" were kept in mind but they were not allowed to impede the relaxation of tension between the two blocs. Critics of a too eager Ostpolitik claimed that the West's willingness to negotiate so soon after August 1968 meant that the Soviet Union "could eat her East European cake and have her Western détente too."[49]

In May 1970 the Soviet Union signed a new treaty with Czechoslovakia which underscored the concept of "limited sovereignty" for socialist states.

The preamble to the treaty confirmed that "support, strengthening, and protection of socialist achievements are an international duty, common to socialist countries." Gromyko praised the treaty as "a step forward in the elaboration of the norms of international law, a new type of relations between socialist states."[50]

Western resignation to the fact of Soviet domination in Eastern Europe did not, and does not, signify a lack of hope or belief in the eventual assertion of national autonomy in Eastern Europe and the eventual success of pressures for political liberalization like those that accompanied economic development in the West. In fact, a "mirror image" of peaceful competition had emerged for both superpowers because there was no alternative that would not risk a nuclear holocaust. However, that competition was directed increasingly inward. Each opponent half believed and half hoped that a stable international environment would benefit the home team and hurt the opponent. As one observer described this:

> Among blocs, alliances, or regional organizations, rivalry no longer leads to conquest or even to active subversion. It becomes a matter of "competitive decadence," of comparative resistance to the forces of disintegration which eat away at all of them...[51]

The Western nations were trying to analyze how a security conference might affect this "competitive decadence". The immediate reaction was naturally to be highly suspicious of a conference that was strongly favored by the Russians. But to support the "forces of liberalization" which existed in the U.S.S.R. the West dared not a too hard line approach or they would only be confirming the neo-Stalinist expectations. On the other hand, to acquiesce in short term economic understandings and symbolic gestures of good will might only facilitate Soviet military capabilities, create a false sense of détente in the West, and inhibit the transition to economic and political reform in the Soviet Union and Eastern Europe which their faulty, ideologically rigid structures made necessary.

The problem was essentially the same on both sides of Europe. How could one best influence the opponent's internal development and control his external ambitions without frightening him into military build-ups and without damaging one's own alliance structure? Pierre Hassner described the situation this way:

There is thus a two-fold paradox in this current era of negotiations. On the one hand, all this spectacular activity amounts basically to recognizing the status quo. Yet on the other hand, this recognition of the status quo could activate psychological and social forces that would undermine it far more powerfully, because more unpredictably, than all diplomatic or military undertakings now being contemplated.[52]

The fact that such Western strategies as "bridge-building" or "gradualism" were vehemently attacked by the Eastern Alliance may indicate the degree to which the East fears ideological pollution. It may also indicate the success of such strategies whose ultimate aim is, after all, evangelistic, like the appeal of communism. The Western fear of ideological undermining by the socialists in the Third World and in Western Europe is similar to the Soviet fear. The logic of détente may be based as much on balanced beliefs in the feasibility of winning the struggle peacefully as on the balance of nuclear terror.

A difficulty for the conference proposal arose with the misunderstanding surrounding the term "peaceful competition" and its meaning for security. "Some East Europeans…interpret 'security' as encompassing economic and social matters that the West would consider as contributing only indirectly to 'security'…"[53] The concept of "cultural contacts" was added to economic, technical, and scientific contacts as a possible agenda item for the conference by the Warsaw Pact in March 1969, the Budapest Appeal, and by the West in its May 1970 statement from Rome. Tension over the meaning of this item is directly related to the different interpretations of security. To the East, cultural contacts involve strictly controlled expansion of tourism, visits by artists, and other "safe" contacts between East and West. The proposal of NATO for "freer movement of people, ideas, and information" becomes a security threat to the East, an attempt at intervention in their domestic affairs.

One certainly cannot claim that NATO rushed into the European security conference. The flurry of activity surrounding Brandt's Ostpolitik, the beginning of Four Power Talks on Berlin, and the first discussions in SALT I were all mentioned by NATO as positive developments in its communique from Rome in May 1970. NATO did not, however, consider these developments as sufficient justification for a security conference in the near future. Negotiations by themselves were not an adequate "test of the willingness of all interested countries to deal meaningfully with real issues of security", the communique stated. Stressing the need for MBFR discussions, the NATO Ministers again declared that "they were ready to multiply exploratory conversations with all interested parties on all questions affecting peace." For the Ministers, the pre-condition for a conference on European security was evidence in other areas, particularly force reductions, which would indicate Soviet sincerity. The pertinent paragraph declared that:

> In so far as progress is recorded as a result of these talks and in the ongoing talks – in particular on Germany and Berlin – the Allied Governments state that they would be ready to enter into multilateral contacts with all interested governments. One of the main purposes of such contacts would be to explore when it will be possible to convene a conference, or series of conferences, on European security and cooperation. The establishment of a permanent body could be envisaged as one means, among others, of embarking upon multilateral negotiations in due course.

"Progress" in the ongoing talks was the flexible prerequisite whose fulfillment would be determined by the NATO Ministers. Attached to the communique was a "Declaration on Mutual and Balanced Force Reductions". In the Declaration the Ministers recalled the lack of response by the U.S.S.R. to past calls for MBFR talks. They called for the establishment of "active explorations between the interested parties at an early date". These exploratory talks, according to the Ministers, "would provide tangible evidence of the readiness to build confidence between East and West." Noteworthy is the fact that the French Foreign Minister declined to sign the Declaration on MBFR, saying that is was "absolutely unacceptable to the socialist countries".[54]

Despite the loopholes and extremely tentative language, the Rome Communique was a breakthrough for the conference proposal in that at last NATO had declared itself officially in favor of a European security conference. Secretary of State Rogers made more explicit the American position on the conference in a statement to the House Foreign Affairs Committee two weeks after the NATO meeting. Unpersuasively, Rogers declared that the U.S. had no intention of exploiting the rift, grown very rancorous, between the Chinese and Russians. He did mention, however, that the Chinese, with whom the Americans had opened discussions in Warsaw, had cancelled the scheduled May 20 session in protest over the American sortie into Cambodia. (Nixon had made the action known to the American public on April 30.) The Soviets however did not react wrathfully and they did not let the invasion cool their zeal for the security conference. Rogers described the approach to European security favored by the United States, and apparently NATO as well, as a "step-by-step approach". Rogers elaborated:

> Such an approach has already been launched in the West German talks with the U.S.S.R., Poland, and East Germany and in the four-power discussions over Berlin. Talks on mutual and balanced force reductions would be a useful further step.

Rogers went on to underline the American position that the convening of a conference could only come if "there should be a good prospect that the conference would have meaningful results." What would indicate that "good prospect"? "Progress on the talks now going on," which, Rogers said, would be "assessed at our December NATO meeting".

The May 1970 NATO communique appeared to accept the eventual convening of a European security conference, a long-standing Soviet invitation which was first expressed in definite terms by the 1966 Bucharest Declaration. The communications during the years since 1966 between the blocs were official, through a barrage of "communiques" and "declarations", as well as unofficial and discrete, such as those early contacts between the F.R.G. and the East. Also important communications were those unspoken acts such as the invasion of Czechoslovakia and the U.S. commitment to Vietnam or the American opening to China.

The Warsaw Pact responded promptly to NATO's May statement and to Secretary Rogers' remarks with a memorandum issued by the Foreign Ministers from Budapest on June 22. Despite the rather cool tenor of the NATO communique, the Warsaw Pact continued with the "reasonable" approach. For instance, American and Canadian participation at the proposed conference was explicitly invited:

> The question of the makeup of the conference has been clarified – all European states may take part, including

the G.D.R. and the F.R.G. – on an equal footing with each other on the basis of equal rights with the other European states – and also the U.S.A. and Canada.

The memorandum did not deal individually with the various bilateral discussions, which NATO had indicated must show "progress" as a precondition for preparing the conference. The Foreign Ministers did note however, that "It is understood the convention of the conference should not be made dependent on any preconditions". In regard to the oft repeated NATO call for MBFR talks, the Warsaw Pact suggested a third agenda item for the conference. This was the creation of a permanent body to consider questions of security in Europe on a regular basis. The memorandum stated:

...in the interests of a productive consideration of the question regarding a reduction of foreign armed forces, this question could be discussed in the body whose creation at the all-European conference is proposed, or in another form acceptable to the interested states.

This was a far cry from NATO's position that MBFR talks would indicate sincerity for compromise before the conference was convened. In addition, the phrase "foreign armed forces" caused Western analysts to wonder if the Soviets included indigenous forces or forces on the territories of other states or simply non-European forces, i.e. American troops in Europe. Although the May NATO communique had spoken of a "permanent body" in connection with the conference, it referred to it as "one means, among others of embarking upon multilateral negotiations in due course." The Soviets apparently had in mind a permanent organ to exist after it was created by the conference itself.

Despite these differences, the Warsaw Pact memorandum was an advance for the conference proposal because the East finally recognized specifically NATO's MBFR proposals. They instructed the Hungarian representatives in the various NATO capitals to indicate a new willingness on the part of the Eastern bloc to discuss force reductions in Central Europe.[55]

This set of proposal and counter-proposal is evidence of the change over the years in the approach to European security taken by both sides, particularly on the part of the Soviet Union. Rather than "dissolution of the blocs", the emphasis now was on recognition of "existing realities", a recognition which was essential for reasonable discussion, and resolution of the issues which threatened security for both sides of Europe. Acceptance of the U.S. in any future security arrangements for Europe was proof that the U.S.S.R. had at least revised, if not rejected, its belief that offensive splitting tactics directed at the West were the most effective means for gaining influence in Europe. The apparent structural change in the international system, away from rigid bipolarity, was a major reason for this changed perception. The Soviets expected that the concession they made on this point would be met by the West with recognition of the "existing reality", and legality, of the G.D.R. as well as the Russian interests in Eastern Europe generally.

As the time approached for the NATO Foreign Ministers to assess the "progress" in the ongoing negotiations which they insisted must precede preparation of the security conference, these issues were the questions they were considering. They were questions whose answers could only come with time.[56]

1. Would a pan- European security system be any more secure than a Europe divided into military blocs?
2. Under a European security system, what would be the guarantee of security and who would make that guarantee?
3. What role would the alliances play, if any, in the new system?
4. How would a system of collective European security affect the social, political, and economic development of the states of Europe?

In short, the conference idea was dangerous because it would inject a large measure of uncertainty into the logic of détente. It had the potential, however, for a higher level of certainty, and therefore security for the entire world, as well as for Europe. This was its attraction.

Chapter II

Europe Meets at Helsinki

The final clarification of the issue of participation by the Warsaw Pact at its June 1970 meeting in Prague coupled with the first official NATO acceptance of the CSCE* proposal as possibly beneficial set the stage for clearing away the preconditions raised by NATO in its communique from Rome in May 1970. Those pre-conditions were progress on the bilateral discussions between the F.R.G. and Poland, the G.D.R., and U.S.S.R., and progress on the Four Power Talks over Berlin, and some Soviet compromise on the Western MBFR proposal. Meanwhile, the neutral states of Europe stepped up their support for the CSCE. In July 1970 the Austrian government issued a memorandum noting that "being a permanently neutral state situated between the large military blocs," Austria had been in favor of the CSCE "from the start". The Austrians did, however, appear to support the Western emphasis on MBFR as a crucial component of easing tensions in Europe. Vienna was offered as a possible location for the convening of a multilateral negotiations for MBFR discussions or for the CSCE. The following month, Finland, another strategically located neutral state and long-time proponent of the CSCE, sponsored a "European Security Conference for Youth" in Helsinki. Popular opinion in Europe seemed to be increasingly favorable toward the conference proposal. It was left to the statesmen and politicians to clear the path of the political obstacles which still prevented preparation of the conference.

The Soviet Union's leaders believed that perhaps the decisions at the December 1969 NATO meeting to lower the hypothetical threshold for the use

---

* Note: "CSCE" refers to the "Conference on Security and Cooperation in Europe" as the conference was eventually named.

of tactical nuclear weapons in Europe would stimulate more interest among the non-nuclear states, and perhaps even for the nuclear powers, in finding a basis of cooperation with the East on matters of security. The Soviets had long professed to believe in the inevitable escalation to all-out nuclear war should any nuclear weapons be used by NATO in Europe. From the Russian point of view, it was "Atlanticists" in the West, those who wanted to strengthen the ties between North America and Western Europe and perpetuate the division of Europe, who were standing in the way of preparing the CSCE. Moscow hoped to make the Atlanticist argument against the CSCE appear to be based on an irrational hostility toward the U.S.S.R. for ulterior motives. The preconditions stated by NATO concerning Berlin and the F.R.G. Ostpolitik were portrayed by the Soviets as delaying tactics of the Atlanticists who feared that the CSCE would undermine the reasons for Atlantic unity, a unity that benefited economically Atlanticists in the U.S. and in Western Europe. It is probable however that there was some division among the Soviet leadership over how dangerous and obstructive Atlanticism was for Soviet aims in Europe. "Neo-Stalinists" in the U.S.S.R. desired to weaken NATO by continuing efforts at splitting the Americans from Europe with detent diplomacy and manipulation of West European public opinion and by exploiting the economic "contradictions" in the Western alliance. A reform section of the leadership apparently won the day for its position that the United States could safely be included in the trend toward cooperation and détente.[1]

Whether it was due to Soviet diplomacy or through internal change of perception, the most important state in the equation, West Germany, had altered its foreign policy dramatically under the leadership of Willy Brandt and his Social Democratic Party. The lines were sharply drawn for the West German electorate in the fall 1969 election when the Kissinger-Strauss line of the CDU / CSU coalition "conjured up the communist menace and the 'national sell-out' by their opponents in a manner going even beyond the rhetoric of Adenauer in his prime".[2] The narrow victory of the Socialist Party and FDP coalition gave the necessary, if slim, public approval that Brandt needed to forge ahead in his Ostpolitik. His opposition was considerable, nevertheless. Vested interests in the status quo from both halves of Germany manufactured propaganda that provoked and magnified inflammatory incidents and even leaked confidential documents in some cases in the hope of stopping the relaxation of tension.[3] In the F.R.G. considerable pressure came from the refugee and expellee organizations who felt that their homeland was being bargained, or even given, away.

Brandt realized that the legacy of the invasion of Czechoslovakia was an impediment to his policy but he persisted partly because there did not seem to be a rational alternative. The relations between the blocs and the superpowers were becoming increasingly fluid and the F.R.G. could either swim with the tide, even take a leading position, or it could be swept along without control over its direction. Brandt hoped that the increasing strength of the East European states, which would be augmented by easier contacts with the West would make it very much more difficult if not impossible for the Soviet Union to pull off another invasion like that of Czechoslovakia. The trend toward more international division of labor might also lead the U.S.S.R. to loosen its grip on Eastern Europe simply through recognition of self-interest in not jeopardizing necessary trade flows. Before the occupation of Prague, German Ostpolitik had been aimed primarily at the East Europeans minus the G.D.R., and that had worried the Soviets. The new target of Brandt's policy was the Soviet Union itself. Although one commentator described the change as "a slightly inelegant preference for Moscow" after the invasion of Prague, the new strategy soon proved to be more fruitful.[4]

Brandt envisioned a new European security system in which both superpowers would participate. The system would be built through renunciation of force or the threat of force agreements, balanced force reductions, and other confidence building measures. A European security conference would be part of the process. The resultant security system could enhance the stabilizing function of the two alliances through some arms regulations and inter-bloc cooperation or it could gradually eliminate the two alliances replacing them with an entirely new system in which all of the European states could participate. Brandt preferred the former projection but he did not rule out the latter.[5] Both directions he felt might finally lead to a "European Peace order" which could progressively eliminate incompatible goals among the states involved in Europe's security. Only under such circumstances would German reunification ever be possible.

The possibility of a CSCE ever being convened was greatly enhanced when Brandt put his policy into action in 1970. The hope was that by dealing directly with the U.S.S.R. first and demonstrating to them that the intent of the policy clearly was not to undermine their society or their relations with Eastern Europe, the Soviets could in turn show flexibility on other issues. More accurate perceptions by both sides of the other's interests and intent made the dialogue possible and productive. Pierre

Hassner summed up succinctly this increased "certainty" which allowed for mutually beneficial change:

> *The Soviet Union feels confident to embark on a "Westpolitik" including Germany precisely because, through her intervention in Czechoslovakia, she has gained recognition for the firmness of her resolve to keep Eastern Europe, if necessary by force. She can gain ground in her dialogue with the West because she no longer presents a direct challenge to Berlin's link with the Federal Republic of Germany, the F.R.G.'s with the Common Market, and Europe's with the United States. Germany can embark on a dynamic Ostpolitik precisely because its substantive content consists of recognizing her division and, on the other hand, because she leaves no doubt on the maintenance of her West European and Atlantic ties and on the need to keep the American military presence in Europe.* [6]

Between the spring and winter of meetings of both the Warsaw Pact and NATO, the F.R.G. signed renunciation of force agreements with the U.S.S.R. and Poland. Events moved so rapidly in 1970 that they took Brandt's opponents in both Germanys rather by surprise. [7]

In support of the treaty with Poland the West German government argued that the F.R.G. was not giving anything away, as Western opponents claimed, since it was impossible to give away what one did not have. The government also hoped through the treaty to undercut Soviet claims of West German "revanchism" which had been used in the past as a cohesive for Eastern European unity. It is also important to note the economic incentives on both sides for normalization of relations as evidenced by a billion dollar trade deal between the F.R.G. and the U.S.S.R, concluded shortly after Brandt signed the Nuclear Non-Proliferation Treaty. The deal called for German pipes in construction of a pipeline across western Russia. In return the F.R.G. was to receive Soviet gasoline.

The "Renunciation of Force and Cooperation Treaty" between the F.R.G. and the Soviet Union was signed on August 12, 1970. It called for further normalization of the situation in Europe beginning from "the actual situation existing in the region". Both parties disavowed "any territorial claims against anybody", with the proviso that a final peace treaty according to the 1945 Potsdam agreement or mutual agreement between states might still change boundaries. The F.R.G. added, importantly, that final ratification of the Treaty by the Bundestag would only come after progress toward a satisfactory conclusion of the Four Power Berlin discussions was evident. The Soviets later made it clear that failure of the ratification process would be considered a dangerous breach of faith. Under pressure from internal groups, the F.R.G. also published unilaterally a supplementary document which promised that the F.R.G. would sign similar treaties with the G.D.R. and Czechoslovakia. But disconcertingly for the U.S.S.R., the supplement also insisted that although the F.R.G. would recognize the G.D.R. on a basis of equality and no longer claim to represent all of Germany, West Germans would not recognize the G.D.R. as a foreign nation, but as a second German state within one nation, thereby hinting that reunification was still a justifiable goal. The Soviet government made it clear that it would respect the letter and the spirit of the bilateral treaty only.[8] The problem was more one of internal West German sensibilities than of some discrepancy over the meaning of the Treaty. The first of the NATO preconditions was surmounted.

While the West Germans were the center of attention in the rush of East-West détente developments of 1970, the Soviets were aware that wider formal acceptance of the partial settlement with the West Germans would make the ratification process in the F.R.G. more certain and also make extension of the agreement more possible.[9] France was a natural place to start. The attitude of the French toward NATO and the United States, though still wary of superpower control, had warmed considerably since the demise of De Gaulle. France had been skeptical of the proposed CSCE because she felt that it might only sanctify the positions of both superpowers in Europe and that there was little to gain for the other European states. France approved of the bilateral contacts outside of the bloc context but they were gradually won over to the idea of a multilateral CSCE by the Romanian leader Ceausescu during his visit to Paris in June 1970. Ceausescu also suggested a standing European security institution under the auspices of the United Nations which might limit the influence of the superpowers. A trip by Pompidou to Moscow in October 1970 produced a joint declaration praising the F.R.G.-U.S.S.R. renunciation of force treaty and calling for "permanent cooperation between all interested states, outside the framework of bloc politics". This cooperation, the declaration stated, would be enhanced by the CSCE. The signatories declared themselves ready to participate in the preparatory work for the CSCE "as much through bilateral contacts as in, at the earliest opportunity, a multi-lateral framework". MBFR was not mentioned.

The following month, November, Finland published an Aide-Memoir declaring its readiness to host the CSCE. The statement was as flexible as possible in order not to elicit a negative response from either side. The Finnish government, the statement declared, "has emphasized that the participation of governments in various stages of the present process of consultation and negotiation does not imply recognition under international law of existing political circumstances in Europe". Careful preparation was essential to insure the success of the CSCE, the Finns stated, and initial consultations by representatives of the states at Helsinki would be "to intensify without commitment the exchange of relevant information. These consultations might enable the governments concerned to obtain the necessary information permitting them to eventually define their position on the possibilities of convening a conference.

Following this offer of neutral sponsorship, the F.R.G. came to a "satisfactory conclusion" in its discussions with Poland. The main issue between the two countries was the recognition of the Oder-Neisse Rivers as the western boundary of Poland. The 1945 Potsdam Agreement stated explicitly that the boundary, which moved Poland westward into territory formerly controlled by Germany, should be provisional until final peace settlement with German was signed. Throughout the Cold War years, West Germany's emphasis on the provisional nature of the boundary brought charges of West German revanchism. Those charges were persuasive to the Eastern Europeans who had so recently experienced Nazi occupation and anti-Slavic Nazi propaganda.

Feelings were also strong in the Federal Republic. Public sentiment against any relaxation of the emphasis on the mutability of the boundary was fanned by expellees and refugee groups whose members came from the territories now under Polish control. But as generation succeeded generation the desire that Germany might someday regain the lost territories waned. "In 1965, a memorandum of the Evangelical Church Council on the question of expellees hit the card houses of Bonn politics like a bombshell. The Oder-Neisse question, the memorandum argued, was not so much a legal as a moral problem and it was about time the Germans faced up to their moral debt toward the Poles."[10] A poll taken of West German public opinion in 1950 indicated that 80% of the respondents were against recognizing the Oder-Neisse boundary. A similar poll taken in 1967 showed that only 33% took that position while over half expressed support for recognizing the boundary.[11]

German statesman Walter Scheel explained the painful change in German opinion:

> *We cannot dispose over something that has long been at the disposal of history; we cannot give up something we no longer possess. To lose one's homeland is bitter, to look on Breslau, Danzig, or Deutsch-Krone as Polish cities is bitter. But if at least after twenty-five years we take note of existing reality, it is not we who have created the reality. The Federal Republic of Germany has to shoulder the burden of the National Socialist legacy.*[12]

Brandt's démarche to Poland, by recognizing the "existing realities", helped to stabilize the territorial status quo in Central Europe particularly in the eyes of the East Europeans. The hope for the West was that this symbolic concession would also bring flexibility to the political relationships between the F.R.G. and the East and perhaps even loosen the authoritarian systems of the communist domestic societies.[13] Despite the enthusiasm which the F.R.G.-Poland agreement received generally in the East, some nervousness remained. While the shift in emphasis was definitely toward acceptance of exiting realities the treaty explicitly reminded everyone that existing agreements were not nullified, that the Potsdam agreement was still in effect, and the division of Germany as well as the Oder-Neisse boundary remained provisional until a final peace settlement. The treaty between the F.R.G. and Poland was also dependent on ratification by the West German Bundestag and the Four Power Berlin accord.

Shortly after the Polish-German accord, the Warsaw Pact published a "Statement on Questions on Strengthening Security and Developing Peaceful Cooperation in Europe". The meeting, which took place in East Berlin, declared that"

> *Sufficient pre-conditions for the holding of such a conference have now been created as a result of the preparatory work already done. The agenda is known in general outline, the participants in the conference have been determined, and*

*a broad basis has been laid for mutual understanding and
for ensuring positive results of the conference….There are no
reasons whatever to delay the convocation of the conference
or to advance any preliminary terms.*

But the Warsaw Pact states also noted "the increasing activity of aggressive NATO circles, ceaseless attempts from the outside to retard the development of favorable processes on the European continent". The Eastern bloc reaffirmed support for the Czechoslovak demand that the F.R.G. renounce the 1938 Munich Agreement *ab initio*, they called for the admission of the G.D.R. into the United Nations, and they warned that without East German participation, an "edifice of lasting peace" could not be built in Europe. It should be remembered however that in order to complete their treaty with the West Germans, the Poles quietly dropped their former positions, despite urging from the G.D.R., that the F.R.G. must first recognize the East German regime formally.

The December NATO Ministerial meeting must have appeared to Soviet hardliners as proof of Western intransigence. The NATO Ministers did not agree with the leaders of the Warsaw Pact that the basis for preparing the CSCE had been established. While the Rome NATO meeting had only called for "progress" on the talks then underway, the December meeting, after the signing of the treaties between the West Germans and Poland and the U.S.S.R., now insisted that the negotiations over Berlin between the Four Powers must come to a "satisfactory conclusion". A stalemate in SALT and problems in the F.R.G.-G.D.R. dialogue also contributed to NATO's stiffening position. On the Berlin issue, the main obstacle to agreement appeared to be the unwillingness of the Soviets to accept all the ties between the F.R.G. and West Berlin which the Western Powers desired. Particularly, the Soviets objected to West Berlin being represented internationally by the Bonn government. Although Manlio Brosio, Secretary General of NATO called the situation after the communique from NATO Ministers "a little standstill with the hope of going forward later", many East Europeans felt it was a step backwards for the CSCE.[14] Indeed, there were rumors, hints dropped by Western statesmen, that NATO might even add conditions concerning the Mediterranean and the Middle East which the U.S.S.R. would have to fulfill before the CSCE could be convened with Western participation. Finally, the NATO Ministers reminded the world of their desire for MBFR discussions and, though not officially making such talks a precondition for the CSCE, they claimed that the Warsaw Pact had "not directly responded to past NATO declarations on the subject". The Warsaw Pact responded in February 1971:

> ...*circles which are not interested in a strengthening of détente in Europe are increasing their opposition to the convening of the all-European conference. This opposition is shown through the suggestion of different pre-conditions governing the convening of the conference and which are aimed at complicating the work of organizing a conference with the other problems, thus placing obstacles in the path of a conference. The decisions of the recent meeting of the North Atlantic Council at Brussels also tend towards increasing the arms race in Europe.*

No mention of MBFR was found in the document. The need for extensive preparation before the CSCE did appear to be conceded however.

President Nixon in his Foreign Policy Report to Congress on February 25, 1971 noted the repeated CSCE proposals by the U.S.S.R. but insisted that "progress on concrete issues" was still necessary to create the "political basis" for the conference. Specifically, Nixon complained, "such conference, in the Soviet formulation, would not address the main security issues – the German question, Berlin, mutual force reductions – but only very general themes".

An important breakthrough came finally at the 24th G.P.S.U. Party Congress of April 1971. The European security conference was given prominence at the convocation. Premier Kosygin suggested the CSCE would lead to all-European cooperation in freight traffic, electric power, the environment, and in the fight against cancer and heart disease. But the important remarks came from General Secretary Brezhnev who, although dusting off the old "dismantle the blocs" rhetoric, did declare Soviet readiness to engage in talks leading toward the reduction of forces in Central Europe. He reaffirmed Soviet readiness two weeks later at a speech in Tiflis, including both foreign and national forces as possible subjects for discussion.[15] Brezhnev's speech at Tiflis came at the same time that the Mansfield Amendment calling for unilateral troop reductions in Europe was being rejected by the American Senate. If the Soviets had hoped to lull the U.S. into a false sense of security by appearing ready to negotiate force reductions, then their plan backfired. With discussions on MBFR becoming more likely, the argument that the strength of U.S. forces in Europe should be maintained as "bargaining chips" when going into the talks won the day in the American Congress.

The NATO Ministers at their June 1971 meeting in Lisbon acknowledged the change in Soviet position:

> *Ministers representing these governments welcomed the response of Soviet leaders indicating possible readiness to consider reductions of armed forces and armaments in Central Europe.*

The communique from the meeting also announced the intent to appoint a representative from NATO to discuss with the Soviet Union and other interested governments the arrangements and agenda for negotiations. In October, M. Brosio, former Secretary General of NATO, was assigned this role but he never received an invitation to Moscow. Although this was construed by the West as a mark of Soviet insincerity toward MBFR, it is more likely that a sole representative from the hostile military bloc was not a negotiating format which the U.S.S.R. wished to sanctify.

The June 1971 NATO meeting, although it did note progress on their MBFR proposal, maintained the necessity of a satisfactory conclusion to the Four Power talks as a prerequisite to the CSCE. The communique stated flatly that when that agreement was reached, "multilateral conversations intended to lead to a conference on security and cooperation in Europe may then be undertaken".

The abnormal situation had been deadlocked until discussions among the four former allies of World War II, the U.S., the U.K., France, and the U.S.S.R. began again in 1969. By mid-1971 twenty-five meetings between the Four Powers had led to several near breakdowns as well as premature announcements of agreement.[16] The East Germans even hampered the process at times by closing down or harassing the access routes to West Berlin.[17] The G.D.R. took the position that West Berlin may be under legal Four Power Control, but in the last analysis it was on East German territory. The Western Powers argued that if East Berlin could be completely integrated into the G.D.R., the F.R.G. should at least be allowed a special relationship with West Berlin. They reminded the East Germans occasionally that under the occupation statutes still in force pending a formal peace treaty: <u>all</u> of Berlin should be under Four Power purview. Although East Germany gained control over the access routes to West Berlin in 1955 when the G.D.R. became officially sovereign, the amount of pressure it could put on the West was limited by its interest in economic exchanges with the F.R.G. and by the political preferences of the U.S.S.R.

By May 1971, the Soviet Union appeared to accept unhampered civilian access to West Berlin, consular representation by the F.R.G. internationally for West Berlin, and freedom for West Berliners to visit relatives in the G.D.R. and East Berlin.[18] The final Four Power Protocol said that traffic in people and goods to West Berlin would not only be "unimpeded" but even "facilitated". The F.R.G. was to continue to maintain special ties with West Berlin but West Berlin could not become a constituent part of the F.R.G. A source of acute tension in the past had been meetings of the West German national political organs in West Berlin. This was forbidden under the treaty. The Soviets were allowed to establish a consulate in West Berlin. Finally, West Berliners, who had been discriminated against in the past, were given the same visiting rights in the G.D.R. as those given to West Germans and other foreign nationals. The implementation and details of these arrangements were left to intra-German arrangements. This historic protocol was initialed on September 3, 1971 to be signed and take effect in June 1972.

The provision that the Four Power Protocol be implemented and supplemented by agreements between East and West Germany was a potentially disruptive qualification. The G.D.R. was displeased by the Four Power agreement because it reasserted Soviet residual rights in East Berlin and over access routes to West Berlin. It was soon apparent that the East Germans were stalling in their discussions with the F.R.G. Meanwhile, the Brandt government of the F.R.G. made it clear that the Four Power Protocol was only a beginning in the process of answering the German questions, but he did declare that because of the agreements there would be no more Berlin crises.[19]

The Western powers made it clear that the intra-German discussions must proceed smoothly or they would not affix their final signatures as scheduled for June 1972. The NATO Ministers stated in a communique from their December 1971 meeting that:

> ….the German arrangements to implement and supplement the Quadripartite Agreement now appear to be nearing

completion, and that, once these arrangements have been concluded, the Governments of France, the United Kingdom, and the United States would be prepared to sign forthwith the final Quadripartite Protocol which bring the complete Berlin Agreement into effect....Ministers recalled that at their meeting in Lisbon they declared their readiness to undertake multilateral conversations intended to lead to a Conference on Security and Cooperation in Europe as soon as the negotiations on Berlin had reached a successful conclusion.

Final ratification of West Germany's treaties with Moscow and Warsaw also waited satisfactory results of the intra-German discussions.

The breakthrough in the relations between the two Germanys took place in March 1970 when Willy Brandt, the new Chancellor of the F.R.G. visited Erfurt, East Germany, accompanied by the Premier of the G.D.R., Willi Stoph. The enthusiastic greeting which Brandt received from the East German crowds, while probably a bit embarrassing for his East German hosts, did not betray the deep-seated tensions between East and West as did the riots by left and right wing demonstrators when Stoph made a return visit to Kassel, West Germany in May. The meetings between the heads of state only ended in agreement that a "thinking pause" was necessary in order to consider how the recognition issue would be handled. The G.D.R. leadership rejected Brandt's "two states one nation" formula as "recognition by the installment plan".[20] Formal negotiations began nevertheless between the two states on November 26, 1970.

The G.D.R. is an extremely important ally for the Soviet Union. It is the U.S.S.R.'s largest trading partner and it boasts the highest per capita income in the communist world. East Germany has a population of only about 20 million people yet it ranked as the world's ninth leading industrial power. But relative to West Germany, the Soviet "sphere of influence" in what was recently a united Germany is much less important or powerful than the Western allied F.R.G. The F.R.G. has nearly twice the territory of the G.D.R. and three times the population. For reasons of inherent strength and types of political relationships, the ties of the F.R.G. and the G.D.R. with their respective blocs are quite different from each other. The G.D.R. leadership has been one of the most hardline anti-Western of the communist countries. This was true under Ulbricht's leadership as well as under the direction of his protégé, former security chief Honecker who replaced Ulbricht at the Eighth

Party Conference in mid-1971. The East German hard line began coming into conflict with the Soviet Union's policies under Brezhnev. Brezhnev's "Peace Offensive" began in 1970 with the aim of normalizing relations with the F.R.G. Soviet actions, including a visit by Brandt to Yalta in the fall of 1971 and Brezhnev's trip to Paris in October made clear that the Soviets would look unkindly on East German obstruction of the path toward the CSCE. Both meetings produced joint statements pledging further efforts at convening the conference at an early date.[21] Peter Merkl describes here the relationship between the U.S.S.R. and its East German ally:

> *The Soviets not only refused to force East German demands upon Bonn, but had even stated their readiness to bring about, on the basis of residual occupation rights, a Berlin settlement to Bonn's liking and presumably at East German expense. The assertion of the occupation rights meant a severe setback to East German pride and self-confidence. The G.D.R. leaders honestly could not tell whether they were being taken to the altar or down the garden path. The nightmare of agreement between Bonn and Moscow had ever been East Berlin's cauchemar des coalitions.*[22]

The relationships between the F.R.G. and its allies were considerably different. The whole process of détente in Europe rested to a large degree with the decisions of the West German government, and people, although superpower détente certainly put great pressure on the F.R.G. The tide was certainly bringing détente for Europe and the superpowers, but the F.R.G. had an important say in how high and fast the tide would rise. In purely legal terms, as enunciated in the Occupation Statutes, recognition of the G.D.R. was not even Bonn's to give. Nevertheless, pressure to maintain Western unity in the recognition of the "existing realities" meant that Bonn's success in reaching a *modus vivendi* with the G.D.R. would have an important impact on Western policy as a whole. Important in this respect was President Nixon's visit to Peking in February 1972 and the announcement of his impending trip to Moscow in May. These developments helped overcome strong opposition from the West German CDU / CSU and progress in the negotiations between Bonn and the G.D.R., as well as in the separate discussions between West Berlin and East Berlin, were achieved. This led to the ratification by the Bundestag of the renunciation-of-force agreements with Moscow and

Warsaw in May 1972. One week before that ratification, the CDU / CSU lost a vote of no confidence aimed at unseating Brandt. Although Brandt won by only two votes, the floodgates were opened. Six months later the Basic Treaty between the F.R.G. and the G.D.R. was initialed.

The Basic Treaty was revealed two weeks before the West German parliamentary elections on November 19, 1972. Popular support of the treaty was demonstrated by a vote giving Brandt's SDP its first outright electoral victory over the CDU / CSU. The Basic treaty called for: (1) Normal, good neighborly relations between the two states; (2) Sovereign equality, self-determination, and protection of human rights in both halves of Germany; (3) Discontinuance of claims by Bonn to represent all of Germany; (4) Promoting European security including arms reductions; (5) Steps toward economic, scientific, and cultural cooperation; and (6) An exchange of permanent diplomatic missions between the two states.

The Basic treaty, signed on December 21, 1972, stated that the F.R.G. "formally takes note of the G.D.R. as a sovereign and equal state", though not as a foreign country as Brandt later pointed out to reporters.[23] Upon completion of the treaty there was a rush of diplomatic recognitions for the G.D.R. as the "Halstein Doctrine" was forever laid to rest. One analyst commented that the chain of events demonstrated that "West Germany still claims a voice in how and under what circumstances, but no longer whether, East Germany should gain international recognition. Its allies continue to recognize that voice".[24]

The United States and the other Western allies heralded the German agreements as significant steps forward in détente and for stability in Europe. President Nixon summed up the importance placed on the negotiations over Berlin and between the two Germanys in an address to Congress on foreign policy in May 1973 saying, "If we could not resolve this one specific issue, there was little prospect of resolving broader security questions." Arthur Hartman, Asst. Secretary of State for European Affairs testified before the House subcommittee for International Political and Military Affairs in 1976 concerning the progress of the CSCE. The Asst. Secretary gave the administration's opinion of the meaning of the East-West agreements of the early seventies:

> *We think the agreements have in fact buttressed our rights*
> *there [Berlin] and have made quite clear certain things that*
> *were fuzzy or had caused some difficulty over the years on*

the original Berlin Agreements in the post war period. We think that this has led to greater stability there. There have not been any serious incidents or buildup of tension in the area. Procedures are established for settling any disputes about the terms of this agreement.[25]

The problems centered around Germany, Hartman went on, were the sources of the greatest tension. Once these were overcome the CSCE could serve a useful purpose. The Asst. Secretary stated that:

....we think [the German tensions] have been dealt with, that relationships have been building up between the Federal Republic and the German Democratic Republic. We waited until after this process had been completed before recognizing the German Democratic Republic which we have now done, so these things were really gotten out of the way before we got to this conference.[26]

Although optimism engendered by the successful negotiations between East and West over the German problems certainly had some legitimate basis, it should be remembered that none of the participants believed the problems were permanently settled. The agreements were only the beginning of the process of normalization of relations as leaders from both East and West were quick to point out. The G.D.R. continued throughout the negotiations to insist that the contrast between the social and political systems of the two Germanys demanded "a sharp demarcation in all matters" between the two legal entities. "International law relationships," an East German official declared, should be carefully scrutinized so that they "could not be construed by the ruling circles of the Federal Republic to represent the allegedly continuing unity of the nation."[27]

MBFR

The NATO allies had explicitly declared that the satisfactory conclusion of the German and Four Power negotiations would have to precede preparation of the CSCE. No such explicit connection was made between the CSCE and the Western proposal for MBFR negotiations. However, as the inter-German negotiations reached their conclusion, the NATO countries began to put more emphasis on the need for MBFR as the critical factor in steps toward greater European security. After the acknowledged position change by the Soviets toward MBFR in early 1971, the Warsaw Pact had become silent on the issue again. The communique from the Warsaw Pact meeting in December 1971 made no mention of MBFR. The NATO Ministerial meeting which immediately followed the Warsaw pact meeting commented on this apparent Eastern reversion:

> *These Ministers noted with regret that the Soviet Government has so far failed to respond to the Allied initiative in this important area of East-West relations in which that Government had earlier expressed an interest….The interested Allied Governments continue to believe that prior explorations of this question are essential in preparation for eventual multilateral negotiations.*

U.S. Secretary of State Rogers in an address to the NATO meeting advocated a bloc approach to any MBFR discussions or CSCE and he called development of a common line in the West prior to any negotiations. This was a situation that the Soviet Union hoped to avoid. Further expressing the implicit connection between the MBFR and the CSCE, Dr. Joseph Luns, Secretary General of NATO, warned the Soviet Union that without agreement "to talks on force reductions, either at the Conference or at a separate meeting, no East-West discussions would have great significance".[28]

A Warsaw Pact statement issued from Prague in January 1972 at last returned to direct pronouncements on the MBFR proposal. Although still objecting to the bloc-to-bloc format favored by the West, the Pact did declare its willingness to negotiate on the reduction of national forces as well as foreign forces in Central Europe. Returning to the Brandt-Brezhnev formula enunciated at Yalta in 1971, the statement declared that no reductions should be "to the detriment of any of the countries taking part".

President Nixon dealt with the proposed CSCE at some length in his report on foreign policy to the Congress in February 1972. Nixon stressed that the conference would only be valuable if it addressed the substance and not the shadow of tension between East and West:

> *If such a conference is carefully prepared and will address substantive issues, the United States favors it. It is in the*

longer term interest of the Soviet Union, too, I believe, that
a conference be used productively in this way and not merely
a forum for speeches and friendly atmosphere. It is essential
that we have a clear picture of what issues a conference can
address and what concrete contribution to security it can
make.

President Nixon's meeting with General Secretary Brezhnev in Moscow in May 1972 provided the discussion which signaled at least that multilateral preparation of the CSCE would begin. This historic meeting, preceded by Nixon's opening to China and the obvious implications of that for the Soviets, produced several documents and substantive agreements. One document was entitled "Basic Principles of Relations between the United States of America and the Soviet Socialist Republics". This document listed twelve points by which the superpowers agreed to conduct their relations. The points covered were general in nature such as the need for mutual consultation and information, avoidance of accidents which might produce tension, and cooperation in non-military fields. A second document contained an elaboration of these points. This joint-communique contained the following paragraphs side-by-side giving an indication of the close connection between the CSCE and MBFR in the discussions:

The U.S. and U.S.S.R. are in accord that multilateral con-
sultations looking toward a Conference on Security and
Cooperation in Europe could begin after the signature of the
final Quadripartite Protocol of the agreement of September
3, 1971. The two governments agree that the conference
should be carefully prepared in order that it may concretely
consider specific problems of security and cooperation and
thus contribute to the progressive reduction of the underly-
ing causes of tension in Europe. This conference should be
convened at a time to be agreed by the countries concerned,
but without undue delay.

Both sides believe that the goal of ensuring stability
and security in Europe would be served by a reciprocal
reduction of armed forces and armaments, first of all in
Central Europe. Any agreements on this question should
not diminish the security of any of the sides. Appropriate

agreement should be reached as soon as practicable between the states concerned on the procedures for negotiations on this subject in a special forum.

Summit meetings to be successful require a great deal of advance preparation. Under the glare of publicity even in spite of preparation the heads of governments may feel it is necessary to appear inflexible and resolute, for domestic audiences. The executives also usually lack the technical expertise to negotiate the fine points of important issues. However, the summit meeting may have the advantage of pressuring both sides to reach some accord lest their failure be magnified by the media into a confrontation. Also, there is the possibility that the heads of government might develop a personal rapport and with the authority immediately at their disposal they can cut through red tape and details which had held up negotiations at lower levels. It may well be that Richard Nixon developed such a personal rapport with Leonid Brezhnev.

In addition to the agreements to begin preparations for the CSCE and for MBFR talks, the two leaders signed a treaty limiting permanently the development of anti-ballistic missiles and putting a temporary ceiling on offensive strategic missiles. While Soviet newspapers stressed the importance of the summit meeting for the European situation and the convening of the CSCE, the American press emphasized the SALT I agreement. President Nixon later however acknowledged the importance of the 1972 summit meeting for the CSCE:

> *A conference might be appropriate if individual countries succeeded in regulating their relations and resolving some of the territorial and political issues. This was accomplished by West Germany's treaties with the Soviet Union and Poland, the Quadripartite Agreement on Berlin, and the SALT agreements. At my summit with the Soviet leaders in May 1972, I agreed that we now could begin preparing for a European conference with the aim of broadening European cooperation….Not until the Berlin and SALT agreements were concluded in 1972 was it possible to work out a sequence for beginning negotiations in separate forums on a Conference on Security and Cooperation in Europe and on a mutual and balanced force reductions.*[29]

As negotiations began to expand into a multilateral framework, it became important to coordinate purposes and strategies among the various issue areas for both blocs. Pierre Hassner commented that it was the success of Ostpolitik and SALT, two very different sets of discussions, which led to their mutual Europeanization. The CSCE, MBFR, and SALT II presented more areas of overlap and potential confusion therefore demanding more inter-bloc coordination.[30]

The Western and particularly American pattern in their détente strategy has been to link political détente with concrete examples of that détente through arms reductions or even simple self-restraint in arms production and development and in the use of force world-wide. NATO Secretary General Luns described this strategy as "parallelism":

> *In exploring possible systems leading towards a military détente, we may learn whether political détente is to last. This is why allied governments have insisted on parallelism between the discussion of the political and military aspects of security. Soviet acceptance of this parallelism has been a major success of Western diplomacy. Of course, talks on Mutual and Balanced Force Reductions will be highly complex and will outlast, probably by years, any European Security Conference.*[31]

There is a great deal of speculation as to the Soviet motives for their agreement to participate in MBFR discussions. The most obvious one, for the purpose of this study, was to get Western attendance at the CSCE. The possible value of the CSCE for the U.S.S.R. has been described earlier. A second motive attributed to the Soviets is that they may hope that through the MBFR process to intervene in the relations among the NATO members exploiting the differences of opinion. Relationships within NATO between the U.S. and Western Europe had become a little acrimonious after the Nixon surprise dollar devaluation of August 1971, his surprise trip to Peking, and the unsurprising American balance of payments problem aggravated by U.S. troops in Europe. In his address to Congress in 1973 Nixon noted that the U.S. deficit due to its forces in Europe was 1.5 billion dollars in 1972. As the President explained to Congress:

> *The Europeans have thus been pursuing economic regionalism, but they want to preserve American protection in*

*defense and an undiminished American political commit-
ment. This raises a fundamental question: can the principle
of Atlantic unity in defense and security be reconciled with
the European Community's increasingly regional economic
policies.*

By beginning MBFR talks, the Soviet Union may have hoped to encourage further squabbling over a burden that would appear even less
essential in light of Soviet "political" détente.

Cost is a factor for the Soviet Union as well as for NATO in the issue
of force reductions. The U.S.S.R. increased its military manpower by 30%
since 1964 and vastly increased its nuclear arsenal. There are approximately
400,000 Soviet troops in Central Europe compared to 191,000 Americans.[32]
Economic pressures, which are granted as possible reasons behind Soviet
desires to make trade and technological deals with the West, also pressure
the Soviet leaders to distribute spending into areas of the economy more
productive and politically popular than armaments.

Another possible motivation for MBFR discussions from the Soviet
point of view is to stabilize the Western front in the face of the growing
Chinese problem. Troops "reduced" in the West might be relocated to
the Chinese border. In addition, the MBFR might encourage the U.S. to
give more favor to the U.S.S.R. in the new triangular situation created by
Nixon's trip to China. This adds another facet to the MBFR substantive
issue because the question is raised, what is to be done with reduced forces?
Could the Soviets send them to Southern or Western parts of the U.S.S.R.
from Central Europe where they could more easily be re-introduced than
American forces returned across an ocean? Should troop reductions actually be totally demobilized?

Finally, many analysts feel that Soviet troops perform an important political function in Eastern Europe. The argument that the function of Soviet
troops in Eastern Europe is different from the function of American troops
in Western Europe is based in the belief that the most important reasons
for the U.S. troops are as tangible evidence of American support in a totally
defensive Alliance and as proof of Atlantic unity in international relations,
particularly vis a vis the East. On the other hand, the main reason for Soviet
troops is to provide backing for the unpopular communist regimes of the
Warsaw Pact states and as a constant reminder of the limitation of those
states' sovereignty and security. The essence of the whole argument is that

American troops are desired by the West Europeans while Soviet troops are unwanted by both the governments and the people of Eastern Europe, seen practically in the role of military occupier. The validity of this image is questionable. The Eastern Europeans, with the occasional exceptions of Poland and Yugoslavia, have also been cool to the Western MBFR proposal. Whether this is because of skepticism of Western intentions behind MBFR or because they feel bound to follow Soviet policy is difficult to know for certain. The Yugoslavs are somewhat apart from the other East Europeans, obviously. They feel that MBFR will enhance their security against both sides but they object to bloc-to-bloc negotiations as only strengthening the superpowers' position in Europe.

Even if conducted on a bloc-to-bloc basis, the East Europeans could gain some political maneuverability through MBFR if they made another invasion like the one in 1968 more difficult for the U.S.S.R. Again, this complicates the negotiations by making the reliability of Eastern European forces suspect in their loyalty to the U.S.S.R. The Soviets may only feel secure with large numbers of Soviet troops at forward positions and may be unwilling to bargain them away even though equivalency between the blocs in Central Europe could be maintained by indigenous troops.

The French government opposed MBFR primarily because bloc-to-bloc talks as NATO desired would, they felt, only perpetuate the political division of Europe. Michael Debré, a French politician and statesman, made this statement on MBFR and CSCE:

> *On even numbered days, meetings for the defense of Europe, encouragement from the United States to the European nations to increase their military budgets and their armies! On odd-numbered days, meetings for security in Europe and discussion on troop reductions, to which the United States consents – it could not really do otherwise since elsewhere through discussions on strategic arms limitation, which it wants to be successful, it is obliged to keep the door open to a reduction in certain types of forces in Europe. The tendency to link the Conference on Security and Cooperation in Europe with the reduction of forces – a tendency that France has denounced – will increase the difficulty...If we are not careful soon no one will have much idea where so-called Western diplomacy is leading Europe.*[33]

Debré and the French believe that if MBFR is only symbolic, it will collapse of its own illogic as nations refuse to take increasing cuts in troop strengths. But they fear that if the cuts are real, it would make a change in the "relations between forces" which would be, at least, premature.[34]

The leadership of the United States realizes the dilemma in trying to maintain the "essential security policies" of NATO while also believing in and encouraging a relaxation of tensions between East and West.[35] The argument runs that one must maintain strength, and even predominance, in order to negotiate successfully and without fear of subterfuge. The U.S. concurs with the U.S.S.R. that MBFR should not change the balance of power in Central Europe or make any participant less secure than before MBFR.

It is often postulated that one fatal assumption of the arms control method for insuring the peace is in the erroneous belief that political tensions which lead to armaments can be disconnected from questions of reducing those armaments. Nations will disarm if they still feel secure, which must mean that the nature of the political tensions has also changed. Arms control projects of the past have failed to prevent war because the disconnection between arms and politics cannot be made. However, current advocates of MBFR do not try to separate military and political issues by separating MBFR and the CSCE. Just the opposite, they insist on the connection between military and political tensions. This is the relationship of the two sets of discussions, the CSCE to deal with political problems and general security, while the specific military problems involved in MBFR will reflect, prove, and perhaps even encourage progress on political problems. To underrate the value of MBFR as the Soviets and French do is a mistake. But to overrate it, as the NATO countries, particularly the United States, have done, is also the wrong strategy.

Preparations for the CSCE Begin

NATO in its May 1973 communique acknowledged fulfillment of its preconditions on East-West negotiations and formally "agreed to enter into multilateral conversations concerned with preparation for a Conference on Security and Cooperation in Europe". They accepted the 1970 offer of the Finnish government to host the preparations. The talks agreed to were not to be the actual Conference but only the preparations for the Conference. As the NATO communique stated, the preparation was necessary "to insure that their proposals were fully considered at a conference and to establish that enough common ground existed among the participants to warrant reasonable expectations that a conference would produce satisfactory results". The implication was that the Conference might die at the preparatory stage if Western interests were not recognized. Later in the communique NATO added that MBFR talks should begin "as soon as practical either before or in parallel with multilateral preparatory talks on a conference on Security and Cooperation in Europe".

American policy towards Europe had taken on a more assertive posture since the East-West agreements in 1970 and 1971 as well as the Nixon "shock" of August 1971 when the U.S. made it clear that it would not hesitate to use its strength in economic competition with its allies. The West Europeans on the other hand had become less ambitious in their Ostpolitik after the earlier French and German overtures to the East. Feeling growing impotence after the Nixon-Brezhnev summit of May 1972 which gave the CSCE and MBFR their crucial impetus, the West Europeans may have wanted to recapture the initiative in East-West relations through bilateral approaches to the U.S.S.R. in the atmosphere afforded by the CSCE and MBFR.[36] But American leaders have tried to use the multilateral negotiations to strengthen NATO unity. This was described by Deputy Secretary of State Rush in May 1972:

> *By working together in CSCE and MBFR, we are now giving the Alliance a new sense of common purpose, a new set of objectives. This is vitally important at a time when our relationship is being challenged by economic strains and suspicions of unilateral dealings with the Soviet Union. Allied unity in these two negotiations is strengthening the overall Atlantic relationship and enhances its ability to deal with other economic and political strains.[37]*

The United States nevertheless persisted in its efforts at superpower dialogue, perhaps feeling a sort of responsibility as the most powerful of the Western nations. The dual role as defense chief and chief negotiator played by the U.S. leads to rather incongruous actions. In order to impress on the Soviets the steadfastness of American objections to Soviet control in Eastern Europe, Nixon visited two of the most recalcitrant East European states, Romania and Yugoslavia, in 1969 and 1970 respectively. Romania, whose internal communist policies are very orthodox, was granted a comprehensive scientific and cultural exchange with the U.S. in December 1972. In the summer of 1972, Secretary of State Rogers signed a consular convention with Hungary on a trip to Budapest which cleared up long-standing U.S. claims against Hungary for expropriations of American property. These overtures to politically restive East European states is unsettling for the Soviets even as U.S.-U.S.S.R. détente proceeds, just as West European dealings with Moscow cause concern in Washington. Superpower direct negotiations have the advantage of avoiding these concerns over bloc disunity to some degree. The super powers were both aware that the CSCE and MBFR could be disruptive for bloc unity if bloc approaches to the discussions could not be maintained.

The Soviet Union took the initiative in September 1972 in proposing a timetable for beginning exploratory talks and subsequent negotiations on MBFR and a parallel CSCE.[38] NATO agreed that preparation for the CSCE would begin in Helsinki in November 1972. Preparatory discussions for MBFR negotiations were to begin in Vienna in January 1973. These preparatory meetings were to determine the agenda and the times and locations of the actual conference.

The formal ratification of the Basic Treaty between the F.R.G. and the G.D.R. in December 1972 was greeted enthusiastically by the U.S.S.R. even though the CSCE preparations had already begun. The NATO Ministers at their meeting in Brussels in December also noted that they were now ready to support the applications of the two Germanys to the United Nations. So, with CSCE preparations under way and MBFR preparatory meetings soon to begin, 1972 ended with the "era of negotiations" emerging into full multilateral momentum. But Brezhnev, in his speech on December 21, 1972 on the fifty-fifth anniversary of Russian Revolution, sounded a warning note. He stressed that "much will depend on the course of events in the immediate future, and in particular on the turn in the question of ending the war in Vietnam". And on the sensitive issue of human rights, which commentators in the West were already raising as a quid pro quo issue for U.S. attendance at a CSCE that would "ratify boundaries" for the Soviet Union, Brezhnev had this to say:

> *One often hears that the West attaches importance to cooperation in the cultural domain and, especially, to exchange of ideas, broader information, and contacts between*

nations. Permit us to declare here in all earnest: we too are in favor of this, if, of course, such cooperation is conducted with respect for the sovereignty, the laws, and the customs of each country, and if it promotes mutual spiritual enrichment of the peoples, greater confidence between them, and the ideas of peace and good neighborliness.

The CSCE Begins

As preparations for the CSCE progressed in early 1973 some analysts criticized the intense "preparatory" negotiations as being in fact the substance of the Conference itself. Preliminaries to test whether a conference might produce satisfactory results were criticized by a Western analyst as follows:

> ….*[preparation to assure that satisfactory results will be achieved] seems to mean that a basic condition for the security conference is that the security conference will not really be necessary. For, if the success of the conference is granted beforehand, then of course the conference itself can only be justified because of the fact that it was necessary to arrange it in order to make it possible to have such preparations as made it necessary.*[39]

Indeed, the Eastern participants apparently envisaged a brief preparatory session which would produce a general statement on agenda items leaving detailed negotiations for the CSCE proper.[40] When NATO came prepared with detailed agenda proposals, the East was somewhat unprepared. The change to an aggressive Western approach to the CSCE had been in planning since the Conference became more and more likely in the early seventies. While the Eastern states had taken the initiative in the proposals for the CSCE, NATO had not adopted a united position either opposing any conference, or in favoring a conference or series of conference, or even on the possibility of establishing an institution as an alternative to a conference.[41] Many in the West argued that the Warsaw Pact had scored a propaganda victory because of NATO's failure to counter their conference proposals with a Western scheme of equally impressive proportions. It appeared that NATO was uninterested in promoting pan-European security. This argument was part of the reason behind NATO's aggressive opening at the preparatory meetings.

After their initial surprise at NATO's elaborate preparations, the Eastern bloc accepted the need for extensive preparatory discussions. It was agreed that the CSCE would consist of three stages. The first would be an opening session at the ministerial level. That would be followed by detailed negotiations in various committees dealing with specific agenda points. The Soviet Union in the preparatory sessions gave qualified acceptance to Western proposals for the exchange of persons and ideas and for confidence building measures as agenda topics.[42] Brezhnev in his December 1972 anniversary speech anticipated that the actual Conference would begin in the middle of 1973. President Nixon in an address to Congress in May 1973 stated that preparations had made satisfactory progress and that the CSCE would begin that year. Both were right, as the initial meeting of the foreign Ministers of thirty-three European states and the U.S. and Canada met at Helsinki from July 3 to 7, 1973. This was Stage I of the Conference on Security and Cooperation in Europe.

The East immediately made it clear that it would not make concessions simply to speed the Conference along. At the opening session of Stage I the Warsaw Pact states presented their initial positions for the agenda items in Stage II which was to begin at Geneva in September 1973.

> *East Germany and Hungary produced an elaborate document on economic, scientific, technological, and environmental cooperation. Poland and Bulgaria covered the project of cultural relations and exchanges of information. Finally the Czechoslovakian draft reintroduced the proposal for the establishment of a permanent consultative committee. Thus the ground already covered during the preparatory consultations was to be retracted and struggled over again in Geneva.[43]*

Throughout the negotiations in Stage II the exact form which Stage III would take was an open question. Stage III was meant to be a short meeting at an appropriate level to accept the work produced in Stage II. The Soviets hoped that the "appropriate level" would be a summit meeting of the leaders of the states participating. Such a meeting would lend great political weight to the final document. However NATO, lest they be trapped into a grandiose ratification of Stage II conclusions with which they were not completely satisfied, had not officially accepted a summit meeting for Stage III until one month before Stage III actually occurred in Helsinki on August 1, 1975. However, it appeared that during the Nixon-Brezhnev talks in Moscow in July 1974 the U.S. unofficially accepted the summit third stage of the CSCE.[44]

Two other events added to the auspicious beginning of the CSCE in July 1973. First was a visit by Brezhnev to the United States in June 1973. That trip resulted in an agreement between the U.S. and U.S.S.R. on measures for the prevention of nuclear war. Second was the successful conclusion of the preparatory MBFR talks in Vienna on June 28. MBFR substantive negotiations began in October 1973.

These bilateral and multilateral discussions and agreements between East and West along with the CSCE and many other less headline-grabbing contacts were parts of the process of détente which was given an important boost by the initiative of Willy Brandt's opening in 1969 and 1970. The follow-up to Brandt's openings was successfully undertaken by Nixon and Kissinger. Along with the "pieces of paper" which are the symbolic milestones of détente, tangible changes were also taking place. Among these were the relaxation of the Berlin restrictions, exchanges of ethnic Germans from the East to the F.R.G., curtailment of ABM programs by the superpowers, and expansion of the United Nations to include the two Germanys. Although this study focuses on the CSCE and its particular problems and meaning, it is important to keep in mind the larger, often intangible "atmosphere" of détente which made a CSCE possible.

Diplomatic history indicates that there is a direct relationship between the prior preparation of an international conference and the probability of success of that conference. By this criterion, the CSCE did well. Diplomatic history also shows that there is an inverse relationship between the number of participants at a conference and its expectation of success.[45] Here the CSCE appeared to be quite a challenge. Thirty-five nations participated. (See addendum for lists of original signatories and current OSCE membership.) The official languages, though not nearly all those represented at the CSCE, were English, French, German, Italian, Russian, and Spanish.

Some of the critics of the CSCE argued that such a large convocation was unnecessary since many of the outstanding issues were bilateral or quadrilateral in nature and if negotiated in a narrower forum highly sensitive issues could be more fully explored with a greater chance of success. But other analysts argued that the CSCE would stress the over-all nature of European security which bilateral or four-power discussions could not settle. From this perspective it was the low key, long term impact of the

CSCE that was most valuable.[46] There were some early proposals for a small preparatory group such as the four members suggested by Hungary consisting of Belgium, the Netherlands, Hungary, and Poland. This group would have at least worked out an agenda for the Conference. Another suggestion was a "troika" consisting of two bloc associates and a neutral state to make the more perfunctory preparations and to consolidate bloc positions. But these ideas died early in the face of opposition from France, Romania, and others who argued that all interested states should participate. This led inevitably to adoption of the decision-by-consensus rule for both the preparatory sessions and the CSCE negotiations themselves. Each participant had the power to hold up the entire Conference.

In light of this it is remarkable that the CSCE was able to accomplish anything at all. But the general agenda was broad and agreed upon fairly quickly. Three general areas or "baskets" were each assigned to a committee which was then subdivided into sub-committees dealing with more specific points. Basket I covered security matters. It had three sub-committees. The first was charged with "considering and stating in conformity with the purpose and principles of the United Nations those basic principles which each of the participating states is to respect and apply in its relations with all other participating states irrespective of their political, economic, or social systems, in order to ensure the peace and security of all the participating states".[47] This subcommittee eventually drew up the "Declaration on Principles Guiding Relations between Participating States" which preceded all other sections of the Final Act. The second sub-committee of Basket I dealt with military confidence-building measures. A third sub-committee negotiated positions concerning peaceful settlement of disputes.

Basket II was concerned with economic, scientific, technological, and environmental cooperation. This Basket had five sub-committees. One concerned with commercial exchanges, another examined industrial co-operation and projects of common interest, a third studied scientific and technological cooperation, a fourth dealt with environmental problems, and a fifth sub-committee was set up as a catch-all for dealing with issues which did not fit neatly into one of the other four groupings.[48]

Basket III dealt with increased human contacts, the flow of information, and cooperation in cultural and educational contacts among the participants. Here there were four sub-committees, one each for problems in human contacts, information, exchanges in the field of culture, and exchanges in the field of education.

A coordinating committee was created to organize the day to day operation of the Conference. It was also to consider any possible follow-up to the CSCE. The question of follow-up was often referred to as Basket IV although it was not considered on the same level with the other substantive committees particularly since NATO made it clear that it would only consider a follow-up agreement after it had been assured of satisfactory results from the other committees.[49] U.S. Asst. Secretary of State for European Affairs Arthur Hartman described as follows the negotiating process in the CSCE committees:

> .....There are 35 countries involved and you must achieve agreement of all participants on a text. What happens is that various texts are submitted to committee. The committees look them over, and try to narrow the differences. When they cannot narrow the differences they usually bracket parts of them. The text will then continue to circulate with large numbers of brackets and in some practically the whole text is bracketed. The committees continue to go over these texts and try to change the words until they can achieve agreement by all participants on a text...the text is emerging gradually out of the removal of these brackets.[50]

It was agreed from the beginning that the negotiating sessions would be closed to the public thus shielding much of the give-and-take at the Conference from public scrutiny. However, delegates did gradually begin to speak fairly freely about what was going on and where their governments stood on various issues, but they declined to be identified by name and country lest they be accused of violating the confidentiality agreement.[51] From such sources it is known that certain military security measures in Basket I and the issue of freer movement of people, ideas, and information dealt with in Basket III were the last negotiations to be completed.

What the participants hoped to get out of the Conference varied considerably from state to state. Some of the smaller states who are members of one of the military alliances as well as the neutral states hoped to gain some political maneuver room against their larger neighbors. Some states, such as Greece and Turkey, were reluctant about the Conference for a reason just the opposite of a desire for political maneuver room. Being so close to the Soviet Union they were particularly sensitive to Soviet pressure and they felt that the CSCE had the potential for antagonizing the U.S.S.R. and harming détente if NATO adopted a hard line policy. Those two countries also were preoccupied with their dispute over Cyprus, an issue which the CSCE could not solve, and it almost caused Greece and Turkey to withdraw from the Conference. Yugoslavia's position was the epitome of a nation in the middle at the CSCE. Asst. Secretary Hartman noted that the Yugoslavs "made it quite clear throughout the Conference that they are acting independently, that they do not follow either bloc; if anything that they have their own views and that they are going to express them. They have been responsible in several cases for key proposals that have been made and indeed the final compromise proposals when that has been necessary".[52] The importance of non-aligned Yugoslavia, which borders Albania, Greece, Bulgaria, Romania, Hungary, Austria, and Italy was underlined by President Ford's visit to that country and its leader, Josep Tito, immediately following the summit meeting Stage III of the CSCE. On his way there Ford also stopped in Romania, further demonstrating American determination to keep open the process of normalizing relations with the communist countries that were most deviant from the Soviet foreign policies.

The motives of the larger members of the military alliances were also somewhat divergent. This brought strong pressure from the superpowers for coordination within the alliances of positions and negotiation strategies for Stage II. Asst. Secretary Hartman admitted that the United States and been less optimistic about the CSCE than the West Europeans. Hartman explained:

> *The running of the Conference has been largely in the hands of the Europeans who have been more anxious to have this kind of Conference dialog with the Eastern countries and the Soviet Union. I think there has been a feeling among many of the West European states that as the détente process developed and as the United States and the Soviet Union had their own bilateral discussions and dialog, that somehow or other Europe was being left out. Therefore they were anxious themselves to have some process in which they would participate and in which they would be able to deal with some of concerns that they had.[53]*

One example of the studied American nonchalance toward the CSCE was the decision not to have a person of ambassadorial rank representing

the U.S. in Stage II until late in the proceedings when the American ambassador to Czechoslovakia went to Geneva to represent the United States.
The U.S.S.R., in contrast, always had an ambassador present and at times
as many as three Soviet ambassadors were in Geneva simultaneously.

West European associations such as the Council of Europe, the North
Atlantic Assembly, and the European Economic Community (EEC),
expressed interest in the CSCE but their effect on the proceedings was
marginal since the United States, although cool toward the CSCE, still was
very important in the coordination of positions. Membership limitations
of the various West European organizations limited their ability to effectively participate. NATO was by far the most influential grouping for the
West. But simply coordinating the American position was a complicated
undertaking. The people involved for the United States in organizing the
negotiations for Stage II varied from issue to issue as Hartman described:

> For example, on the economic subjects we have a commit-
> tee that is composed of ourselves in the State Department,
> the Special Trade Representative's Office, Treasury, and
> Commerce. On the military confidence building measures
> we have a committee that is composed of the NSC staff,
> Defense, and ourselves. On the other items, which are more
> strictly within the purview of the State Department, we have
> the Inter-Office Committee. The major positions are all put
> to the Secretary of State for his decision.[54]

As in the United States, West European opinions on the potential of
the CSCE varied considerably, though they were generally more optimistic.
Some West Europeans feared that the CSCE might lead to a kind of regional
security system excluding the U.S. which would have adverse consequences
for Western Europe, i.e. they envisioned the "Finlandization" of Europe.
Others argued in favor of the CSCE that there were already existing and
growing bilateral ties between the East and West and that further bilateral
"bait" thrown out by the U.S.S.R. might hurt Western unity. A multilateral
conference at which the West could adopt a concerted policy might prevent
the dangers of bilateralism.

The EEC was particularly interested in forming a common position
which could further enhance their political unity and force the East to deal
with them as a legitimate entity. The Nine were not formally represented at

the CSCE, the participants being restricted to recognized sovereign states. The Eastern bloc had pursued a policy of non-recognition of the EEC for ideological and political reasons. However, Romania's request in February 1972 to be included among the less developed countries who receive special preferences from the EEC, in addition to several speeches by Brezhnev calling for equal relations between the EEC and Comecon, indicated that Eastern policy toward the EEC was moderating. A European Parliament working document on the CSCE contained this statement:

> ...it is noteworthy that neither the Soviet Union nor other Warsaw Pact or Comecon members have challenged the right of the Nine to speak and act collectively at Helsinki or Geneva. Thus the Soviet Union and the other Eastern European countries have tacitly recognized the international status of the Nine and their right to act as an entity in international political and security as well as economic negotiations. This represents a major step forward in Community / Eastern European relations.[55]

The EEC coordinated its positions on the issues dealt with in Basket I and III by caucuses of the Heads of Delegations of the member governments before each session. Positions decided upon were communicated by the state that held the EEC Council chairmanship or by one of the other eight members. Most of the EEC's importance was in the position shaping for the economic issues in Basket II. The EEC Commission itself sat at the table in the committee and the sub-committees of Basket II as part of the delegation of the state chairing the EEC Council. The Commission officials were even listed by their EEC titles on the official attendance sheet despite initial objections by the Eastern states. The Nine reminded the East of the agreement during the preparatory sessions that each participating state could fill its delegation as it chose.[56]

Coordination of positions for the U.S., the EEC, and the rest of NATO at the CSCE was done by a caucus of all the NATO members at the Conference site or by discussions in the NATO Council, which periodically set policy for the upcoming round of negotiations.[57] Sometimes when a sticking point was reached in the Conference negotiations NATO countries would appoint one member to speak for all, but all the NATO countries had to approve before any agreement was definite. Western proponents of the CSCE pointed to these coordinating efforts as evidence of willingness and ability of the Alliance members to compromise and reach consensus on specific issues in the interest of Allied unity.[58] If this is true, it was a timely support for Atlantic unity in the face of the economic strains brought on by the Arab oil boycott of late 1973.

Although it was generally considered that coordination at the CSCE among the NATO countries was more difficult than it was for the Warsaw Pact because of NATO's greater size and more voluntary form of association, there were apparently some challenges to the total leadership of the U.S.S.R. in the East. In the middle and late sixties when the Conference was a still a Soviet dream, the U.S.S.R. spoke frequently and forcefully about the need for a CSCE while the East Europeans had relatively little to say.[59] Soviet intransigence on issues raised by the West such as American participation and MBFR caused many neutral states to side with NATO on its preconditions for the CSCE. As the conditions were met, however, the neutral states became strong proponents of the CSCE. The East Europeans, Hungary, Poland, and Romania particularly began to show increased enthusiasm for the Conference as it became clear the Western nations would insist on military as well as political problems as topics for discussion.

Authoritarian decision making structures are considered to be more mobile than democracies in international negotiations. There is no free press to criticize government policies, no powerful electorate that might vote out of office key leaders or groups who must make commitments to long term policies. However, it is also believed that it may be indispensable to Soviet legitimacy to appear as the leader in foreign affairs for the communist world. This puts a different sort of pressure on the Soviet Union to be successful either through cooperation or confrontation in its dealings with the West.[60] That pressure bears on two rather indistinct factions in the C.P.S.U. Politburo. One group favored using the CSCE as a forum for anti-Western propaganda. That group, supported by some military figures, certain harsh press commentators, and led by Shelest and possibly Voronov and Shelepin in the Politburo, continued to issue inflammatory statements despite assurances from Brezhnev and his supporters that progress would be enhanced by a congenial CSCE.[61] The preparatory sessions and Western preparedness stilled much of the neo-Stalinist pressure for exploiting the CSCE by forcing the Soviet Union to take a "business-like" approach to the Conference even before it began.[62] The Brezhnev –led group can argue that with the increased level of security against the West thanks to the massive military build-up in the U.S.S.R. over the past decade and through agreements between the superpowers, the U.S.S.R. can make some political concessions in order to increase Soviet influence in Western Europe and perhaps strengthen their control over Eastern Europe. And against those concessions were stacked the recognition of the G.D.R. which attended the CSCE as a government rather than at a technical or observer level as in past international conferences, as well as Western acceptance formally of the boundaries of Europe. These were counted as major political victories for the U.S.S.R. which came with the CSCE. Finally, the lures of economic and technological gains from an amicable CSCE were persuasive reasons for legitimate collaboration with the West at the CSCE.

Between the convening of the CSCE in July 1973 until its conclusion with the summit meeting of 35 heads of government in early August 1975, events outside Europe threatened to undermine the East-West détente that made the CSCE possible. Most notable was the 1973 October Middle East war. President Nixon's world-wide alert of American troops in response to the belief that the Soviet Union was contemplating sending troops into the Arab-Israeli conflict made many people wonder how dead the Cold War really was. The Arab oil boycott encouraged by the Soviets who were then oil exporters also fanned the flames of East-West confrontation ignited by local hostilities in the vital Middle East. Questions were raised as whether security in Europe, which the Soviets desired, should also be linked to Soviet actions in other parts of the world. Should the CSCE deal with military security in the Mediterranean? Should NATO hold up progress in Stage II to pressure the Soviet Union into backing down in its support for the Arabs?

The Vietnam War, on the other hand, was such an issue for the Soviets and certainly opinions were voiced in the East that is was most unseemly for the U.S.S.R. to be negotiating with the Americans while they waged imperialist war in Southeast Asia. These problems did not, as it turned out, seriously affect the negotiations in Stage II of the CSCE and they waned in importance as the U.S. hurriedly left Vietnam and as the U.S.S.R. lost a great deal of its influence in the Middle East. Apparently, although competition in nearly all parts of the world was still recognized as the existing reality by both sides, the superpowers were willing to limit the friction caused by their confrontation in order to maintain and deepen the détente which existed between East and West since the mid-sixties. In this atmosphere the CSCE progressed to a successful conclusion in 1975 and produced a Final Act, a document, or set of documents, sixty pages long in its official English version, that was to be the basis for further normalization of East-West relations in Europe.

The Final Act

The first point made concerning the Final Act of the CSCE is that it is not a legally binding document according to international law. It is an expression of **intent** such as the Universal Declaration of Human Rights or the United Nations Friendly Relations Declaration. Because it did not have the status of a treaty, the Final Act did not require ratification by the U.S. Senate. The Western nations were particularly concerned that the Final Act should not take on a legally binding status for they maintained that the political and territorial questions regarding Germany could only be settled by a formal peace treaty. In addition, the United States did not want to contradict its formal non-recognition of the annexation of the Baltic States by the U.S.S.R. This non-legal status of the CSCE Final Act was believed to weaken the anti-CSCE argument in the West that the U.S.S.R. was gaining some sort of formal recognition of its hegemony in Eastern Europe. Although the CSCE Final Act does not include legally binding texts, the political commitments behind it are seen as significant by all the participants, particularly after being signed by 35 heads of government.[63]

Principles Guiding Relations

Ten "Principles Guiding the Relations of Participating States" appear in the beginning of the Final Act. These are:

I. Sovereign equality, respect for the rights inherent in sovereignty.
II. Refraining from the threat or use of force.
III. Inviolability of frontiers.
IV. Territorial integrity of states.
V. Peaceful settlement of disputes.
VI. Non-intervention in internal affairs.
VII. Respect for human rights and fundamental freedoms, including the freedom of thought, conscience, religion, or belief.
VIII. Equal rights and self-determination of peoples.
IX. Cooperation among states.
X. Fulfillment in good faith of obligations under international law.

The participating states are to abide by these ten principles "irrespective of their political, economic or social systems as well as of their size, geographic location, or level of economic development". This statement represented a defeat of sorts for the U.S.S.R. which wanted the sentence to read: "irrespective of the <u>differences</u> between their political, economic, and social systems", which would have, the West felt, made the guarantees only East versus West and not applicable within the two camps.

Opponents of the CSCE argue that the Final Act might weaken the United Nations Charter, or that at best the Principles enumerated in the Final Act were superfluous because of their redundancy with the UN Charter. For instance Principle II calling for refraining from the threat of force is explicitly stated in Article II paragraph four of the U.N. Charter. But proponents argued that the U.N. Charter did not prevent the invasion of Czechoslovakia in 1968 or the invasion of Hungary in 1956. A restatement of the principle in the specific European context could not hurt and might make a potential aggressor more considerate of adverse international reaction should it use or threaten to use force. But it must be admitted that there is another reason why this oft repeated principle may be superfluous. The non-use of force has been effect in Europe, at least between East and West, since World War II largely because of the balance of power between the two sides. No agreement could substitute for that situation in the current atmosphere of East-West relations. Principle II has its greatest significance, at least from the Western view point, as it can be applied to relations within the Eastern bloc.

A sticking point in the last months concerned where a phrase permitting "peaceful change" of boundaries should be included. Bonn, supported by the other Western nations, insisted that the phrase be included to allow for the possible reunification of Germany and to offset the Final Act Principle dealing with the inviolability of frontiers. The EEC was also interested in this point so that eventual formation of a political union out of the EEC would not be precluded. Since both the reunification of Germany, which many in the West would balk at, and the unification of a supranational EEC, are unlikely, the Eastern countries probably felt safe in this concession. The provision was included under Principle I pertaining to the rights of sovereignty.

The question of the Baltic States was covered by Western insistence that under Principle IV, the territorial integrity of states, no acquisition of territory by force should be recognized as legal. Since this is how the

U.S. describes the annexation of the Baltic States by the Soviet Union, the document conforms to American policy of non-recognition of that annexation.

The West hoped that the Principles concerning equal rights and self-determination, Principle VIII, and the sovereign equality principle would make the so-called "Brezhnev Doctrine", by which the Soviet Union justified the occupation of Prague, a dead letter. Non-intervention in internal affairs, Principle VI, also appeared to contradict Soviet pressures in Easter Europe.

Non-intervention in internal affairs was also a principle with which the U.S.S.R. was particularly concerned. One paragraph of the Principle states that the participants will "refrain from direct or indirect assistance to terrorist activities, or to subversive or other activities directed towards the violent overthrow of the regime of another participating state". The U.S.S.R. hoped to stymie Western penetration of the East through radio and other media which spewed forth "ideological pollution" by appealing to this principle.

The United States and its allies were successful in adding a Principle dealing specifically with human rights. The Principle states that the participants will act in conformity with the Universal Declaration of Human Rights. According to a "Gist" publication by the U.S. State Department in March 1977, "The statement recognizes human rights as both a legitimate concern in relations between states and a proper subject for discussion between them." The Eastern states have, however, argued that Western insistence on examining human rights as an international issue violates Principle VI dealing with non-intervention. The conflict between these two Principles of the CSCE is basic to international relations and the CSCE could not hope to resolve it entirely. The ultimate sovereignty and independence of states will continue to conflict with the growing interdependence of societies and their different cultures, legal customs, and ideologies.

Basket I

Basket I produced a "Document on Confidence-Building Measures and Certain Aspects of Security and Disarmament". Heavy emphasis was placed on finding ways to avoid the misunderstandings and miscalculations which produce tension and can precipitate war. Confidence-building measures included prior notification of military maneuvers, exchanges of observers at military maneuvers, prior notification of major military movements, and exchanges of military personnel.

The key provision concerned notification of maneuvers. "Maneuvers" means war games rather than actual military operations, but it was such maneuvers that the Warsaw Pact was engaged in near the Czech borders just prior to their occupation of Prague. This agenda point was originally proposed by Canada and later supported by Yugoslavia and Romania. [64] In the early preparatory discussions the U.S.S.R. opposed this as an agenda item but later relented. Negotiations then began over what areas should be covered by the notification procedure, whether or not all of the participating states should be notified or just those adjoining the site of the maneuvers, what size maneuvers should be covered, how much time should be allowed for advance notification, and very importantly, whether notification should be mandatory.

Taking the latter point first, Romania informed the other Conference participants that she was ready to hold out for obligatory notifications.[65] The Final Act did state that notification **will** be given unlike other provisions in the Final Act which only use words like "may", "with due regard", "will endeavor", and "voluntarily".

On the other questions the two Alliances were far apart right into the last months of the Conference. The U.S.S.R. was concerned that the area of notification would reach too far into the territory of the Soviet Union. Original positions on this issue ranged from the Soviet suggestion of about sixty miles from the borders between East and West, thus excluding most of Eastern Europe, to the Western figure of 600 miles, which would have reached East to Moscow and West to cover all of Europe. [66] On the time to be allowed for notification before maneuvers, the U.S.S.R. wanted five or six days while the West proposed 35 to 50 days. On the size of the maneuvers subject to notification, proposals ranged from around 12,000 combined land, sea, and air forces to about 45,000 with the East somewhat higher and the West lower. The Soviet Union did not even officially commit itself to **any** advance notification until June 9, 1975.[67]

It is interesting that an American-Soviet compromise proposal was rejected by the NATO allies as "unrealistic" in the area of advance notification, whereupon the United States joined the other NATO countries in a tougher stand.[68] A compromise proposal by several neutral countries was finally adopted with some minor changes. Notifications were to be made to all participating states (the West would not accept only contiguous states since that would have meant the U.S.S.R. would only be notifying its allies of maneuvers on its European territory). Combined forces of 25,000 troops or more were to be subject to notification. Maneuvers covered included those anywhere in Europe, and, if applicable, in the adjoining air and sea space. In the case of countries with territory extending beyond Europe, notification is mandatory only if the maneuvers take place within 250 kilometers from the frontier adjoining any other European state. However, if the maneuver area is contiguous to a non-European state or non-participating state, notification is not mandatory. Twenty-one days was the agreed upon advance notice time. For all these complicated agreements, the impact of this provision is largely psychological, at least in an East-West context, since electronic and satellite surveillance makes secret maneuvers of this size highly unlikely. For intra-bloc relations, the agreement has more potential importance as indicated by the Romanian interest. By 1977 NATO observers had attended some Warsaw Pact maneuvers but no Eastern countries had sent observers to witness NATO maneuvers.

NATO considered other possible agenda items in Basket I, such as arms sales to developing countries, observation posts in each other's territories, and discussions on military doctrine on a regular basis among the participants. The Final Act makes only a short general statement that disarmament would strengthen military security and lessen the chances of confrontation. By the time of the summit meeting the U.S. was officially denying any formal linkage between the CSCE and progress in MBFR talks going on in Geneva. [69] One interesting paragraph notes that security in Europe is related to worldwide military security and particularly to security in the Mediterranean area. A document was included in the Final Act which expresses the signatories' intent to work with the non-participating countries around the Mediterranean for security and cooperation in that area.

Basket II

The largest section of the Final Act covers "Cooperation in the field of Economics, of Science, and of the Environment". This section of the negotiations was the easiest area for agreement between East and West. Observers at Geneva felt that one of the main restraints to even better progress on Basket II was the negative spillover from disagreements in Baskets I and III.[70] The basic assumption behind the efforts at increasing East-West trade and scientific exchanges is the functionalist belief that cooperation in those areas of "low politics" will spill-over into other areas more directly related to security such as arms reductions. It also assumes that economic linkages between East and West will make both sides more cautious in their foreign policies lest they upset advantageous economic relationships. As the first paragraph of this Final Act document states, the participants were:

> ....convinced that their efforts to develop cooperation in the fields of trade, industry, science and technology, the environment and other areas of economic activity contribute to the reinforcement of peace and security in Europe and in the world as a whole.

A steady decline in the annual growth rate of the Soviet Union economy since the 1950s was believed to be the source of Eastern eagerness for economic agreements, and even perhaps the wellspring of détente itself. Western businessmen also saw advantages for themselves in developing trade ties with the Eastern bloc. This was even truer for the West Europeans than for the Americans. The possibilities for co-production schemes taking advantage of large labor forces in the East combining with Western capital and know-how seemed particularly attractive. Lately, however, the labor supply in the East, particularly for skilled labor, and capital investment from the West, has faltered in the aftermath of the oil crisis.

The United States seemed on the verge of a break-through in economic relations with the U.S.S.R. after signing the U.S.-U.S.S.R. trade agreement in October 1972. If it had been approved as it was initially presented to the Congress, the agreement would have granted Most Favored Nation (MFN) status to the U.S.S.R.[71] This agreement, which was another result of the Nixon-Brezhnev summit of May 1972, was to be implemented by Congress through passage of the 1974 Trade Act. However, the Jackson-Vanik amendment was added to the trade Act by Congress. This amendment requires that a country wishing MFN status must demonstrate to the American Congress that it allows free emigration to its citizens.[72] The Soviet Union rejected this stipulation, labelling it "meddling in internal affairs". The Final Act only mentions that MFN treatment could have beneficial effects for the development of international trade. Asst. Secretary Hartman made clear to the House Sub-committee on International Political and Military Affairs "that while the wish is expressed that trade be conducted on a most-favored-nation status, there is nothing that commits us to move by any other way of implementation than by our Trade Act". [73] Despite the political restrictions on mutually advantageous trade, American companies have made some inroads to the Soviet market. For example, in 1976 50 million bottles of Pepsi Cola were sold in the U.S.S.R.[74]

Basket II was very wide-ranging. All of the text is based on voluntarism and is an expression of intent. Among the many issues which receive attention in the Final Act were facilitation of business contacts and improvement of facilities, industrial cooperation, projects of common interest, harmonization of standards, encouragement of arbitration methods when disputes arise, technology sharing in areas such as energy, agriculture, environmental protection, space research, public health, tourism and migrant reforms.

Who benefits most from East-West trade is a matter of opinion. Many in the West argue that West is in effect financing the Soviet military build-up. Others argue that the terms of trade have been favorable to the West and that "linkages" theory for promoting peace makes trade between the East and West valuable no matter who benefits the most economically. The Soviet Union will certainly increase its trade with the West Europeans and thereby its political influence. The U.S.S.R. might also increase its influence with Eastern European economies by conducting the pattern of East-West commercial exchanges. On the other hand, if it cannot control that pattern, the U.S.S.R. may find the economies of the more advanced East European states such as Czechoslovakia and the G.D.R. attracted away from the Soviet Union toward the benefits of Western technology. This is more likely to happen, proponents of the CSCE argue, if the Soviet Union is prevented from "conditioning" East-West exchanges by making these exchanges more normal and of increasing volume. The EEC in particular felt that it had gotten satisfactory results from its participation in Basket II of the CSCE. A European Parliament working document states:

> It is in concerting joint policies toward all the major issues arising at CSCE that the political process of the Nine has proved more successful than in dealing with any political problems so far. Also, at the CSCE the U.S.S.R. and its Warsaw Pact allies have tacitly recognized the Nine to be their interlocateur valable in dealing with major problems of East-West economic cooperation.[75]

Basket III

The famous Basket III is entitled "Cooperation in Humanitarian and in other Fields". Its four sub-sections deal with human contacts, information, co-operation and exchanges in the field of culture, and cooperation and exchanges in the field of education. Romania, which had diverged from the Eastern bloc on other issues in the CSCE, sided with the U.S.S.R. in its opposition to over-emphasizing human rights at the Conference. Because of strong opposition from the East, some of the Western desires for Basket III provisions were not fulfilled. Nowhere in the document appears the phrase "free flow of people, ideas, and information" as the West wanted, although much of the substance of the concept is incorporated in the text itself. The West also wanted the Final Act to rule out radio jamming. The East has periodically tried to jam the Western radio stations "Radio Free Europe" and "Voice of America". The West does not try to silence Eastern European radio broadcasts. But the Final Act only expresses the hope for continued dissemination of information by radio "to meet the interest of mutual understanding among people".

Working conditions for journalists was another sticking point in the negotiations that was not resolved until the final weeks. [76] Agreement was finally reached to grant multiple entry and exit visas for journalists, to ease travel restrictions within countries, to increase opportunities for journalists to communicate with their sources, and to enable them to communicate with their home countries more easily. Reports from Western reporters in the U.S.S.R. have indicated that working conditions for Western journalists have improved noticeably. The Final Act does, however, allow for the expulsion of journalists as long as the offender is apprised of the reason for the action. An incident in early 1977 involving an American correspondent expelled from the U.S.S.R. because he was meeting with Soviet dissidents was countered by expulsion of a Tass correspondent by the United States. As Asst. Secretary Hartman noted, "Here we are negotiating especially sensitive issues for both East and West, partly because the subject deals with 'ideological coexistence', which has always been anathema to Moscow".[77] There are some who would argue that it has been anathema to the West as well. Certainly all will agree with Frederick Hartmann however when he calls for "realism" in expectations of what can and cannot be achieved in changing human conditions in Eastern Europe.[78]

The Final Act of the CSCE includes in Principle VIII language pertaining to human rights which is similar to the wording of the Universal Declaration of Human Rights and also of the International Covenant on Civil and Political Rights. The Final Act declares that the participants will act in accordance with these earlier documents. The NATO countries were careful to make it clear that the Final Act in no way attenuated those documents but that it would instead supplement and add to their provisions.[79] The importance of the human rights section of the Final Act is that it is included in a highly political document dealing with peace and security. It confirms the belief that human rights and their implementation are matters of international concern because they have an effect on peace and security as well as being valuable in and of themselves. [80] Constant repetition of accepted behavior by states in the field of their domestic human rights has the effect of reinforcing those concepts as customary norms of law, national and international. Therefore the violation of those norms becomes increasingly attention-getting and embarrassing for the offending government.

In addition to the value of repetition, Basket III gives a great deal of specificity to what are usually expressed only as general principles of human rights. Specific areas for reform are indicated in which states can increase the flow of information between states and increase human contacts. Early agreement was reached on provisions calling for facilitation of family reunification, family visits, marriages between nationals of different states, and access to information.[81] This was particularly important to West Germany. In 1975, while at the CSCE, Poland and the F.R.G. signed an agreement whereby Poland would allow some 120,000 ethnic Germans to move to the Federal Republic over the next four years. Agreements on further emigration are to be concluded when the current agreement runs out in 1979. In return, the F.R.G. paid $50 million in pension claims dating to the Nazi years and granted credits to Poland worth over $800 million.[82] Since the agreement, over 2,000 ethnic Germans have left Poland each month for the F.R.G. The second largest flow of immigrants to the F.R.G. comes from the U.S.S.R. In the first seven months of 1976 nearly 7,000 arrived in West Germany from the Soviet Union, twice the number allowed to emigrate in the same period of 1975. And in 1977, F.R.G. Chancellor Schmidt, during the uproar over President Carter's human rights statements, claimed that quiet diplomacy in that area had been most effective, citing as evidence the 60,000 East Germans who have been allowed to immigrate to the F.R.G. since the CSCE. [83] West German officials have attributed the general increase in emigration from the East to the West to the efforts on the part of the Eastern governments to comply with the provisions in the CSCE Final Act.[84]

Standing Institution

The issue of whether or not to create a standing institution to carry on some pan-European function after the CSCE was not resolved until the final weeks of the Conference. The delay was caused by Western insistence that the question of a standing institution should not be considered until its utility could be judged by the outcome of Stage II of the CSCE. The possibility of such an institution was actually first suggested by NATO in its communique from Rome in May 1970. However, NATO's proposal, which was rather imprecise, at that time envisioned a committee whose purpose would be to set up a Conference or series of conferences rather than an institution to exist after the CSCE. A month later, in June 1970, at its meeting in Budapest, the Warsaw Pact proposed creation of some permanent machinery with an existence of its own apart from the CSCE. This was suggested as a third agenda item for discussion in the CSCE.

Although the proposal by the Warsaw Pact was at first supported by Belgium and by the U.K. until the Labour Government was defeated in 1970, the NATO countries soon adopted a very cool attitude toward the idea of a permanent institutionalization of the East-West dialog. There were four main arguments why the West should balk at the creation of a permanent institution. First, such a body might allow the U.S.S.R. to dominate Europe politically because of its much greater size and military power in relation to the other European states individually. This would be particularly true in the event of American disengagement from Europe, perhaps precipitated by an American public that believed the standing institution meant less need for U.S. involvement. Secondly, the standing institution might lead to creation of a new European security system that would make NATO unnecessary and give the U.S.S.R. an opening into Western security discussions. Third, the EEC was particularly concerned that the Comecon countries would try to use such an institution to replace the process of economic integration in Western Europe with some form of all-European integration. [85] Finally, many in the West were of the opinion that there were already enough institutions in which follow-up measures could be handled such as UNESCO, the U.N. Economic Commission for Europe, GATT, the OECD, the Council of Europe, or some expansion of the Inter-Parliamentary Assembly to an East-West Assembly. It was argued that governments had not gone very far in exhibiting the potentials of these extant institutions. Ceausescu, the Romanian First Secretary, had suggested that a standing body might be created under the auspices of the U.N., but the predominance of the Western permanent members in the Security Council made the other East Europeans skeptical of that proposal.

Original positions on the issue found the West Europeans and the United States in favor of a waiting period after the CSCE before another conference would be convened. This was proposed formally by Denmark on behalf of the EEC states and endorsed by the U.S. The proposal called for a probationary period until 1977 when a meeting of representatives of the participants would review implementation of the CSCE decisions and consider further follow-up activities.[86] For the East, a proposal was forwarded by Czechoslovakia to establish a committee with a permanent secretariat to carry on the dialog on the issues covered by the CSCE and to prepare further conferences. The U.S.S.R. had, however, cooled on its advocacy of a permanent institution when it became apparent that what the West Europeans feared about Soviet influence through such an institution might instead be reversed to the advantage of the United States. They did not want to institutionalize the American presence in Europe through a permanent CSCE follow-up nor did they want Western kibitzing on Eastern application of the human rights provisions of the CSCE. Undoubtedly, the Soviets were concerned, in the reverse of the fears of Western sceptics, that a standing institution might invite Western intrusion into Eastern security affairs. Also, the strong interest in permanent machinery expressed by Yugoslavia and Romania suggested a tribunal to which the smaller countries of Europe, particularly Eastern Europe, might take their grievances.

In the end, it was the Western concept that was incorporated into the Final Act. Implementation of the provisions of the Final Act is to be carried on unilaterally and bilaterally where necessary, and multilaterally by meetings of experts and in existing institutions such as UNESCO and the U.N Economic Commission for Europe. The East-West convocations initiated by the CSCE are being continued at a review conference in Belgrade, Yugoslavia. That conference began on June 15, 1977. These are preparatory meetings to arrange the date, duration, and agenda of the substantive follow-up itself, projected to begin in October 1977. A $27 million conference building was constructed in Belgrade for the meeting. [87] The problems facing any institutionalization of the CSCE are forbidding. They are similar to those that the EEC has faced, such as the form of the institution, supra-national authority, voting procedures, representation, scope of concern, etc.

The change in attitude of the West toward the follow-up machinery is important for the impact of the CSCE on détente between East and West. NATO Secretary General Luns put it simply, saying that "NATO, because it is defensive in military terms, can well afford to be on the political offensive." [88] The West now views the follow-up as a chance to solve the dilemma of the past which was the need to recognize the status quo in Europe while at the same time opening up opportunities for positive change.[89] A standing institution could bring increasing contact between East and West and lead to more cooperation in all the areas designated by the Final Act. Enforcement of the provisions will not be the purpose of the follow-up, though the West would like to use it as a public forum in which they could point to areas where the East has failed to comply with the Final Act, particularly in the area of human rights. For the East, this potential difficulty is magnified by an increase in internal dissent after the widespread publication of the Final Act in Eastern newspapers. (The Final Act states that, "The text of this Final Act will be published in each participating state, which will disseminate it and make it known as widely as possible.") An unofficial group formed by dissidents in the Soviet Union to monitor Soviet compliance with the Human Rights provisions, along with the "Charter 77" published in the West by Czech dissidents calling for more human freedoms in accordance with the CSCE Final Act are examples of the problems facing Eastern governments. Even the Yugoslavs have faced more pressure from political dissidents which could be embarrassing for them at the follow-up preparations in Belgrade. The hopes for a CSCE follow-up that does not degenerate into a battle of charges and counter-charges of violating the Final Act are summed up by this comment from a top Yugoslav official:

> *For us, the Final Act of Helsinki means much for peaceful development in Europe based on the principles of sovereignty, non-interference and mutual cooperation in all fields. It means for us that the final document is not a partial document. It means overcoming the existing division in Europe. So we respect this document very much and will stick to it as an integral thing, a whole thing, equally. The point is not to interpret it partially for convenience. If there is more peace and security in Europe, we can expect more human rights.[90]*

Conclusion

The Conference on Security and Cooperation in Europe did not put an end to the tension and fear that existed between the capitalist and communist halves of Europe. But did the CSCE help alleviate those tensions? Whether one answers positively or negatively the position is largely unprovable. The ideas of security and détente are abstract notions. Their presence is a matter of perception. For example, the addition of new weapons to an arsenal may be seen as benefitting security because it strengthens one's defenses. On the other hand, it could be argued that the new weapons increase paranoia and produce an arms race that might make war more likely, i.e. a decrease in security.

Because of this difficulty in saying precisely how the relations between the two halves of Europe have changed due to the CSCE, it would be more useful to summarize the desired results, or perceived benefits, of the Conference for the participants. To some degree, each of the participating states had different motivations for attending the conference. But rather than go through the entire list of states individually from the superpowers to Luxembourg and the Vatican, for the purpose of brevity it would not be too misleading to divide the participants according to East and West, or NATO and the Warsaw Pact. Of course neutral states such as Yugoslavia, Sweden, and Austria had particular interests, which were somewhat different from those of the bloc states, but the issues which divide Europe are best illuminated by examining the motivations of the states in NATO and the Warsaw Pact. There were some important differences within those alliances and they will be reviewed.

Most of the reasons behind attending the CSCE were different for the East and the West. When the motivations of the two blocs conflicted, the motivation of one side corresponded to a risk for the other side. There were some important motivations shared by both blocs. These similar interests may have encouraged compromise on the interest conflicts that held up the Conference.

Western Motivations

When the Soviet Union and its allies began their campaign for a CSCE, NATO ignored the proposals. As those proposals became less grandiose, eliminating appeals for dissolving the military alliances, neutralizing Germany, etc., and as they picked up neutral support, NATO developed its own counter campaign. The West insisted that negotiations on specific problems in East-West relations should begin before considering CSCE. Once those negotiations did begin, NATO insisted that they should come to successful conclusions as proof that a CSCE might have beneficial results. This meant that solving the specific issues enumerated by NATO was a motivation for NATO attendance at the CSCE. If the Eastern states wanted the CSCE badly enough to negotiate faithfully on narrower issues, the CSCE idea was valuable to the West as a kind of bait for Warsaw Pact flexibility in these earlier negotiations.

1. Berlin – The Four Power Protocol clarified the status of the city that had been the source of a great deal of tension in the past. As described in Chapter 2, there were reasons for both alliances to be happy with the agreement.

2. The renunciation of force treaties between the F.R.G. and the U.S.S.R., Poland and Czechoslovakia ended the uncertain territorial policies stemming from the F.R.G.'s non-recognition of the Oder-Neisse boundary line, met Czechoslovakia's demand that the F.R.G. renounce the Munich Agreement of 1938 *ab initio*, and undercut the Soviet claims that the F.R.G. was implacably hostile to the Eastern states. This was a risk for the Soviet Union because it had used West German revanchism in the past as a rallying cry for the Warsaw pact.

3. MBFR – NATO's emphasis on arms control as a crucial part of the security in Europe finally forced Eastern acceptance of the MBFR proposal before the CSCE could begin. MBFR posed risks for both sides if the reductions upset the perceived military balance in Europe. It also presented potential benefits for both sides if arms

costs could be reduced and limitations were placed on the abilities for both sides to wage an aggressive war in Central Europe. The immediate effect of the negotiations was to stop the unilateral withdrawal of American troops, a benefit for the West Europeans and a cost for the Soviet Union. In the long run MBFR might allow the U.S.S.R. to shift more military resources to the Chinese border. The Soviet Union also risked losing some military leverage on the East Europeans if MBFR brought a reduction of Soviet troops in the other Warsaw Pact states.

4. SALT – Limiting the strategic arms race has obvious advantages for both sides. Although the SALT I was not made a specific pre-requisite for the CSCE, it coincided with the "go ahead" given the Conference by Nixon in his meeting with Brezhnev in 1972. SALT appeared to be the only extra-European issue with some fairly close connection to the CSCE. Neither NATO nor the United States publicly linked Soviet behavior in other parts of the world to the CSCE proposal.

5. The prerequisites that NATO made for the CSCE were to some degree expressed for counter-propaganda purposes. This was another Western motivation for accepting the CSCE proposal, i.e. to win back their image of flexibility in their policies toward the East as it appeared to the neutral and non-European states. It may well be that Brezhnev believed that the propaganda value of the CSCE proposal was risk-free. Either the West would not accept the proposal or if it did the Conference could be staged so that it would benefit the East. However, as the neutral states and the East Europeans warmed to the CSCE idea, Brezhnev may have been caught in a trap of his own making when the West finally picked up the gauntlet shortly before the CSCE actually began.

6. Western businessmen saw advantages in trade with the East and they exerted pressure on their governments to normalize relations. This was truer for the West Europeans than for the Americans. A relaxation of tensions and more trade agreements could come from a CSCE many Western businessmen believed. This presented a risk to the regimes in the East if business contacts exposed Eastern businessmen to bourgeois influences. Most business is therefore conducted with Eastern government officials closely regulating the contacts. This Western motivation is part of the belief that

"linkages" can be made in the area of economics that will temper any aggressive inclinations the Warsaw Pact might harbor. In addition, the EEC hoped that the CSCE would bring explicit Eastern recognition of its existence as a legal and viable entity.

7.   The Western states hoped that a CSCE would produce a relaxation in the East's policies on emigration, travel, cultural contacts, and the accessibility of information. This appeared to be primarily a humanitarian motivation although it was not viewed as such by the Eastern states. To them it was a risk connected to the CSCE if the West could use the Conference to force some Eastern deregulation in those areas. Subversion and ideological perversion were the hazards.

8.   The West hoped that once the Conference began they could make some agreements that would tangibly enhance their security and inhibit the Soviet Union's ability to threaten West Germany or Yugoslavia or even its own allies. This was the intent for the West in the Final Act provisions dealing with notification of maneuvers and exchange of observers, and in the Principles concerning use of force, non-interference, and sovereign rights. The Eastern European states, particularly Romania, shared this motivation with the NATO countries.

9.   Finally, in more abstract terms, NATO was probably drawn to the CSCE in the interest of détente as a whole. The danger of confrontation in a nuclear world, increasing demands and instability in the Third World, and even environmental concerns may all have swayed Western opinions in favor of the CSCE.

Eastern Motivations

The Soviet Union suggested a pan-European security scheme as early as the mid-1950s but they were usually transparent plans for one-sided gains. As the proposal lost its rough edges in the atmosphere of détente, the U.S.S.R. under Brezhnev's direction maintained its desire for the Conference despite Western prerequisites. Not until during the CSCE itself did the Soviets show signs of hesitation. Even then however, they still appeared to attach more importance to the proceedings than did the United States. It is very important to consider the attitudes of the East Europeans toward the CSCE in relation to Soviet attitudes. The decline in Soviet enthusiasm was apparently related to the increased expectations of its allies for more national autonomy to be guaranteed by the CSCE. The differences within the Warsaw Pact seemed to be greater than those within NATO, although this may be only a Western perspective.

1. Recognition of the territorial status quo was a motivation common to all of the Warsaw Pact states. This goal was partially fulfilled by the bilateral treaties with West. The West as a whole risked the possibility that in the CSCE's Principle of inviolability of frontiers or the Principle concerning sovereign rights the U.S.S.R. would try to read a Western acceptance of Soviet hegemony in East European politics. This was a risk for the allies of the Soviet Union as well. The smaller members of the Warsaw Pact probably hoped that the CSCE provisions concerning sovereignty and non-interference would make more difficult direct Soviet pressure on their foreign and domestic policies.

2. Similar to the idea of recognizing the status quo, the CSCE would give greater legitimacy to the international status of the G.D.R. When the CSCE proposals were first forwarded, the Conference held the prospect of being the forum in which Western recognition of the G.D.R. would finally come. Although that recognition came earlier with the signing of the Basic Treaty between the two Germanys, the CSCE was the first international conference between East and West at which the G.D.R. sat as an equal with the other states. The risk for the West was primarily born by the F.R.G. because recognizing the G.D.R. presented more legal barriers to any eventual reunification.

3. In the first CSCE proposals it was clear that the Soviet Union wanted only Europeans to attend the Conference. The Soviet motivation for a CSCE was to use the Conference to divide the Atlantic Alliance. As it became certain that the West Europeans would insist on American participation, the Warsaw Pact relented, perhaps in anticipation of a NATO concession in return. The East may have continued to believe that the CSCE would lull the Western Europeans into lowering their defenses and into feeling less need for American military support. This was exactly the risk feared by NATO, i.e. losing or appearing to lose, its *main raison d'être* if a CSCE resulted in pan-European security structures.

4. Integration in Western Europe is also viewed by the Warsaw Pact as a threat. Eastern hopes that the CSCE could slow EEC integration were the mirror image of the EEC desires for recognition from the CSCE. The Soviets hoped that through a CSCE, EEC integration would become a secondary priority and ultimately be forgotten in favor of some looser all-European economic framework benefitting the East. The EEC however, believed that the Conference negotiating process itself had strengthened the member states' ability to coordinate policies in areas of "high politics". In the case of either NATO or EEC disharmony, the Soviet Union could expect to increase its influence in Western Europe. Because the United States was particularly sensitive to this risk, NATO and American official statements always stressed the need for unity in the CSCE negotiations, and in other East-West negotiations, above all other considerations.

5. Stabilizing the Western front in the light of a growing Chinese threat may have been another Soviet motivation. This also could have been a factor in the Warsaw Pact's acceptance of the MBFR proposal.

6. The Soviet Union is believed to be very desirous of Western technology and capital. The CSCE presented a possibility of increased access to these things for the East either through the Final Act provisions concerning cooperation in science, technology, and economics, or indirectly by relaxing tensions and thereby loosening Western purse strings as well. The risk here for the West is that it may be financing a Soviet military build-up or supporting communist regimes whose ideologies make their economies inefficient. Another risk for the West may be from the overextension of credits to defaulting Eastern states resulting in harm to Western economies.

7. Broadly speaking, the CSCE, if it becomes a regular feature of European international relations, might be a conduit for the Soviet Union to increase its intervention in the affairs of Western Europe, economically, politically, and militarily. Of course there is reason to believe that the Soviet Union might be concerned about just the reverse situation coming out of the CSCE.

8. Finally, the U.S.S.R. and its allies may believe that the CSCE can strengthen détente and make less likely a disastrous war between the blocs. Avoiding nuclear war, protecting the environment,

helping the Third World economically while containing conflicts there are common interests of the superpowers, although in the latter concern differences in preferred solutions often bring them into conflict.

The prospects of the CSCE for enhancing security and cooperation in Europe and for continuing the progress toward normalizing relations between the capitalist and communist states will depend on how the participants try to use the agreements to fulfill the motivations that brought them to Helsinki. Although it may seem that too many of the motivations ascribed to the two blocs are diametrically opposed for them both to use the CSCE beneficially for their respective interests, it may nevertheless be possible. Success is largely a matter of perception. For instance, in the field of economic cooperation, the West may believe that increasing trade ties facilitated by the CSCE indicate an opening up of the Eastern regimes and perhaps even some liberalization of Eastern economies. At the same time, the East may believe that the increase in economic exchanges resulting from the CSCE gives them greater influence in Western Europe and draws Western Europe away from American hegemony.

Some of the "uses" of the CSCE have already been realized by the completion of the pre-CSCE negotiations. The allies of the superpowers may have taken away from the Conference an increased sense of independence and respect from their respective bloc leader. Even if this is only psychological, it is still an important result of the CSCE and probably beneficial for European international relations.

The prospects for the CSCE depend as much on the tactics selected by the participating states for using the CSCE Final Act as on their ultimate motivations. Although they would like to use the CSCE to fulfill the motivations listed above, they have a wide range of specific policy choices, each of which might bring an unexpected response form the other side. The human rights issue is a case in point. The West would like to see the Final Act provisions concerning human rights used as a pressure on the Eastern states to force them to liberalize. However, it is uncertain whether Western governments should publicly and regularly chide the East for failure to comply with those provisions, or whether it would be better to keep quiet and avoid embarrassing the East into exactly the opposite direction, to rely instead on the peoples in Eastern Europe to demand their own rights according to the Final Act. The U.S.S.R. might wish to use the Final Act to extend its influence in Eastern Europe and to rebuff Western criticisms by referring to the clauses on non-interference. However, such a policy risks a breakdown in beneficial economic exchanges.

At present, the prospects for the CSCE Final Act being an aid to normalization of East-West relations do not appear good. Tensions between the superpowers have mounted in the last year. However, some of the benefits of the CSCE are still evident. Cultural contacts, emigration policies, access to information, and the various military agreements are all areas in which normalization of relations and benefits to security have been recorded. The review conference presents both potential risks and benefits for both alliances. If the major actors in NATO and the Warsaw Pact can maintain their perception of a safe flow of events in Europe, positive for their national interests, there is no reason why the CSCE could not have been the beginning of the end of the division of Europe. The common interests which provide the foundation for détente must be emphasized rather than the conflicting motivations. For détente to deepen and the CSCE to be beneficial to European international relations, new areas of common interest must be found and explored. Nothing guarantees that this will happen. The leaders of the two alliances can encourage such a process by faithfully trying to fulfill the pledges in the CSCE Final Act. Emphasis should be on the common motivations that led to Helsinki so that both alliances can find satisfaction in the agreements. Stressing unilateral successes cannot promote goodwill. Criticisms for failure to live up to agreements reached in the CSCE must be offset by compliments for successful compliance in other areas.

Addendum - 2015

State	CSCE Signatory	OSCE 2015	EEC 1975	EU 2015	NATO 1975	NATO 2015
Albania		X				X
Andorra		X				
Armenia		X				
Austria	X	X		X		
Azerbaijan		X				
Belarus		X				
Belgium	X	X	X	X	X	X
Bosnia-Herzegovina		X				
Bulgaria	X	X		X		X
Canada	X	X			X	X
Croatia		X		X		X
Cyprus	X	X		X		
Czech Republic		X		X		X
Czechoslovakia	X					
Denmark	X	X	X	X	X	X
Estonia		X		X		X
Finland	X	X		X		
France	X	X	X	X	X	X
Georgia		X				
Germany (F.R.G.)	X	X	X	X	X	X
Germany (G.D.R.)	X					
Greece	X	X		X	X	X
Holy See	X	X				

State	CSCE Signatory	OSCE 2015	EEC 1975	EU 2015	NATO 1975	NATO 2015
Hungary	X	X		X		X
Iceland	X	X			X	X
Ireland	X	X	X	X		
Italy	X	X	X	X	X	X
Kazakhstan		X				
Kyrgyzstan		X				
Latvia		X		X		X
Liechtenstein	X	X				
Lithuania		X		X		X
Luxembourg	X	X	X	X	X	X
Macedonia		X				
Malta	X	X		X		
Moldova		X				
Monaco	X	X				
Mongolia		X				
Montenegro		X				
Netherlands	X	X	X	X	X	X
Norway	X	X			X	X
Poland	X	X		X		X
Portugal	X	X		X	X	X
Romania	X	X		X		X
Russian Federation		X				
San Marino	X	X				
Serbia		X				
Slovakia		X		X		X
Slovenia		X		X		X
Spain	X	X		X		X
Sweden	X	X		X		
Switzerland	X	X				
Tajikistan		X				
Turkey	X	X			X	X
Turkmenistan		X				
Ukraine		X				

State	CSCE Signatory	OSCE 2015	EEC 1975	EU 2015	NATO 1975	NATO 2015
United Kingdom	X	X	X	X	X	X
United States	X	X			X	X
U.S.S.R.	X					
Uzbekistan		X				
Yugoslavia	X					
TOTAL	**35**	**57**	**9**	**28**	**15**	**28**

Index

Bibliography

Books

Birnbaum, Karl E., Peace in Europe, East-West Relations 1966-1968 and the Prospects for a European Settlement, London: Oxford University press, 1970

Brzezinski, Zbigniew K., The Soviet Bloc, Unity and Conflict, Cambridge, Mass.: Harvard University Press, 1974

Davis, Jacquelyn K., Lehman, Christopher M., and Wessell, Nils H., SALT II and the Search for Strategic Equivalence, Philadelphia: Foreign Policy Research Institute Monograph Series, No. 19, 1974

Dornberg, John, Brezhnev, the Masks of Power, New York: Basic Books, Inc. 1974

Gilbert, Felix, The End of the European Era, 1890 to the Present, New York: W.W. Norton and CO., 1970

Goodman, Elliot R., The Fate of the Atlantic Community, Praeger Publishers, 1975

Griffiths, Franklyn, Genoa plus 51: Changing Soviet Objectives in Europe, Canadian Institute of International Affairs: Wellesley Paper, June 1975

Hartmann, Frederick H., The Relations of Nations, New York: Macmillan Publishing Co., Inc., 1973

Hassner, Pierre, Europe in the Age of Negotiations, The Washington Papers. Vol. 1, No. 8, London: Sage Publications, 1973

Howard, Michael, Disengagement in Europe, Baltimore: Penguin Books, 1958

Hunter, Robert, Security in Europe, London: Elek Books Ltd., 1969.

Kennan, George F., Memoirs, 1950-1963, Boston: Little, Brown, and Company, 1972

Korbel, Joseph, <u>Détente in Europe: Real or Imaginary?</u>, Princeton, New Jersey: Princeton University Press, 1972

Mayne, Richard, <u>The Recovery of Europe, 1945-1973</u>, Garden City, New York : Anchor Books, 1973

Mensonides, Louis J., and Kuhlman, James A., eds. <u>The Future of Inter-Bloc Relations in Europe</u>, New York: Praeger Publishers, 1974.

Merkl, Peter H., <u>German Foreign Polices, West and East</u>, American Bibliographical Center, Santa Barbara, California: Clio Press Inc., 1974

Nalin, Y. and Nikoleyev, A., <u>The Soviet Union and European Security</u>, Translation by Progress Publishers, Moscow, 1973

Palmer, Michael, <u>The Prospects for A European Security Conference</u>, London: Chatham House, 1971

Sowden, J,K., <u>The German Question, 1945-1973</u>, London: Bradford University Press, 1975

Spanier, John, <u>Games Nations Play</u>, New York: Praeger Publishers, 1972

Stanley, Timothy W. and Whitt, Darnell M., <u>Détente Diplomacy: United States and European Security in the 1970s</u>, Published for the Atlantic Council of the United States. New York: Dunellen Publishing Co., 1970

Ulam, Thomas W., <u>Soviet Power and Europe, 1945-1970</u>, London: John Hopkins Press, 1070

Zimmerman, William, <u>Soviet Perspectives on International Relations 1956-1967</u>, Princeton, New Jersey: Princeton University Press, 1969

Selected Articles from Periodical Publications

Andren Nils, "European Security Conference: A Swedish Scholar's View", <u>Atlantic Community Quarterly</u>, Fall 1972, pp. 312-320

Beugel, Erenst H. van Der and Kohnstam, Max, "Western Europe and America in the Seventies", <u>Atlantic Community Quarterly</u>, Fall 1972, pp. 295-311

Brosio, Manlio, "Europe and the Atlantic Alliance Today", <u>Atlantic Community Quarterly</u>, Fall 1972, pp. 285-294

Critchley, Julian, rapporteur of the Western European Assembly's Defense Committee, "East-West Diplomacy and the European Interest, CSCE, MBFR, and SALT II", <u>The Round Table</u>, July 1974, pp. 299-306

Debré, Michael, ":The Defense of Europe and Security In Europe", <u>Atlantic Community Quarterly</u>, Spring 1973 pp. 93-118

Gasteyger, Curt, From The German Tribune, "Europe Cool to U.S. Suggestions on Revitalized Charter", Atlantic Community Quarterly, Fall 1973, pp. 319-321

Harned, Joseph, rapporteur; Hadidk, Lazzlo; Klaiber, Wolfgang' Sattler, James; and Wasowski, Stanislaw, "Conference on Security and Cooperation in Europe and Negotiations om Mutual and Balanced Force Reductions", Atlantic Community Quarterly, Spring 1973, pp. 8-54

Korbel, Joseph, "Prospects for Economic and Cultural Cooperation", Atlantic Community Quarterly, Fall 1972 pp. 321-330

Luns, Joseph M.A.H., Secretary General of NATO, "NATO View of Security Conferences", Atlantic Community Quarterly, Spring 1973, pp. 55-64

Rush, Kenneth, U.S. Deputy Secretary of State, "The NATO Alliance: The Basis for an Era of Negotiations"", Atlantic Community Quarterly, Fall 1973, pp. 327-334

Scrivner, Douglas G., "The Conference on Security and Cooperation: Implications for Soviet-American Détente", Denver Journal of International Law and Diplomacy, Vol. 6, No. 1, Spring 1976, pp. 122-158

Radoux, L. Rapporteur, "Report Drawn Up on Behalf of the Political Affairs Committee on the Conference on Security and Cooperation in Europe", European Parliament Working Papers, Doc. 485/74, 21 February, 1975

U.S. Congress, House Committee on International Relations, Hearings before the Subcommittee on Europe, 92nd Congress, 2nd Session, 1972

U.S. Congress, House Committee on International Relations, Hearings Before the Subcommittee on International Political and Military Affairs, 94th Congress, first session, 1975

The following periodical publications also provided information:

Atlantic Community Quarterly

Current Digest of the Soviet Press

Department of State Bulletin, United States

Foreign Affairs

New York Times

Orbis

Radio Free Europe Research Reports

U.S. News and World Report

Washington Post

Footnotes

Introduction and Chapter 1

1   Robert Hunter, <u>Security In Europe</u> (London: Elek Books, Ltd., 1969), pp. 3-4

2   Karl E. Birnbaum, <u>Peace In Europe, East-West Relations 1966-1968 and the Prospects for a European Settlement</u> London: Oxford University Press, 1970, p. 23

3   Y. Nalin and A. Nikolayev, <u>The Soviet Union and European Security,</u> translation. Moscow 1973, Progress Publishers, p. 26

4   Michael Debre, "The Defense of Europe and Security in Europe", <u>Atlantic Community Quarterly</u> Spring 1973, p. 94

5   Karl E. Birnbaum, <u>Détente in Europe, East-West Relations 1966-1968 and the Prospects for a European Settlement</u> London 1970, Oxford University Press, p. 10

6   Joseph Korbel, <u>Détente in Europe, Real or Imaginary?</u> Princeton 1972, Princeton University Press, p. 65

7   Birnbaum, p. 24

8   U.S. Congress, House Committee on Foreign Affairs, "Recent Developments in the Soviet Bloc", Hearings before the Sub-committee on Europe. 88th Congress, 2nd Session, part II, p. 350

9   U.S. Senate, Committee on Foreign Relations, "U.S. Policy Toward Europe (and related matters)" Hearings before the Committee, 89th Congress, 2nd session. P. 161

10 U.S. Congress, House Committee on Foreign Affairs, "The Crisis in NATO". Hearings before the Sub-committee on Europe. 89th Congress, 2nd Session, part II, p. 161

11 Mojmir Povolny, "The Soviet Union and the European Security Conference", <u>Orbis</u>, Spring 1974, p. 207

12 Marshall D. Shulman, "Europe Versus Détente", <u>Foreign Affairs,</u> Vol. 45, No. 3, (1966-1967), p. 391

13 Birnbaum, p. 20

14 Robert Hunter, <u>Security in Europe,</u> London 1969, Elek Books Ltd., p. 8

15 Averell Harriman, <u>Department of State Bulletin</u>, 29 May, 1967, pp. 818-819

16 Zbigniew K. Brzezinski, "Toward a Community of the Developed nations", <u>Department of State Bulletin</u>, 13 march, 1967, p. 418

17 Ibid., p. 418

18 Birnbaum, p. 13

19 Ibid., p. 66

20 <u>Department of State Bulletin</u>, 29 May, 1967, p. 820

21 Korbel, p. 89

22 Thomas W. Wolfe, <u>Soviet Power and Europe, 1945-1970</u> London 1970, John Hopkin Press, quoting Moscow Radio broadcast by Victor Glazunov, 14 December, 1967

23 Birnbaum, p. 18

24 Wolfe, p. 331, quoting <u>Pravda</u>, "Joint Soviet-English Communique", 25 January, 1968

25 Korbel, p. 63

26 "Moscow Opposes Vienna Proposal, Seeks to Exclude U.S.", <u>New York Times,</u> 11 April 1968, p. 84

27 Birnbaum, p. 84

28 Wolfe, p. 414

29 Hunter, p. 118

30 Korbel, pp. 96-98

31 Ibid., p. 98

32 Michael Howard, <u>Disengagement In Europe</u> Baltimore 1958, Penguin Books, p.91

33 Povolny, p. 211

34 <u>New York Times</u>, 14 November, 1969

35 Timothy W. Stanley and Darnell M. Whitt, <u>Détente Diplomacy: United States and European Security in the 1970s</u> New York 1970, Dunellen Publishing Company, p. 2

36 L. Radoux, Luxembourg, rapporteur, "Report of the Conference on Security and Cooperation in Europe", <u>European Parliament - Working Documents</u> 21 February, 1075, p. 9

37 Louis J. Mensonides and James A. Kuhlman, eds. <u>The Picture of Inter-Bloc Relations In Europe</u> New York 1974, Praeger Publishers, p. 75

38 Hunter, p. 425

39 Mesonisdes and Kuhlman, p. 76

40 Palmer, <u>The Prospects for a European Security Conference</u> London 1971, Chatom House, p. 47

41 J.K. Snowden, <u>The German Question 1945-1973</u> London 1975, Bradford University Press, p. 345

42 Ibid., p. 346

43 Mesonisdes and Kuhlman, quoting "Press Conference at the Soviet Foreign Ministry", New Times, No. 4, 1968, pp. 16-17)

44 Povolny,. P. 215

45 Ibid., p. 215

46 Pierre Hassner, "Europe in the Age of Negotiations", The Washington Papers, Vol. 1, No. 8, 1973, p. 72

47 Franklyn Griffiths, "Genoa Plus 51: Changing Soviet Objectives in Europe," Wellesley Paper Canadian Institute of International Affairs, 4 June, 1973, p. 52

48 Hassner, p. 64

49 Korbel, p. 104

50 Griffiths, p. 69

51 Hassner, p. 69

52 Ibid., p. 68

53 Palmer, p. 5

54 Korbel, p. 80

55 Povolny, p. 216

56 Palmer, p. 61

Chapter II

1 Franklyn Griffiths, Geno Plus 51: Changing Soviet Objectives in Europe, Wellesley Paper, Canadian Institute of International Affairs, June 4, 1973, p.40

2 Peter H. Merkl, German Foreign Policies, East and West Santa Barbara, California, Clio Press Inc., 1974, p. 132

3 Ibid, p. 134

4 Pierre Hassner, "Europe in the Age of Negotiations" The Washington Papers, Vol. 1, No. 8, 1973 p.59

5 Karl E. Birnbaum, Peace in Europe, East-West Relations 1966-1968 and the Prospects for a European Settlement, London 1970, Oxford University Press, p. 31

6 Hassner, p. 13

7 63 Merkl, p. 133

8 Manlio Brosio, "Europe and the Atlantic Alliance Today", Atlantic Community Quarterly, Fall 1972, PP. 285-294, 290

9 Mojmi Povolny, "The Soviet Union and the European Security Conference", Orbis, Spring 1974 pp. 201-230, pp. 218-219

10 Merkl, p. 148

11 Ibid., p. 149

12 Ibid., p. 150

13   Joseph Harned (rapporteur), and Laszlo Hadik, Wolfgang Klaiber, James Sattler, Stanislav Wasowski, "Conference on Security and Cooperation in Europe and Negotiations on Mutual and Balanced Force Reductions". <u>Atlantic Community Quarterly</u>, Spring 1973, pp. 8-54, pp. 18-19

14   Michael Palmer, <u>The Prospects for a European Security Conference</u> 1971 London, Chatham House, p. 17

15   Joseph Korbel, <u>Détente in Europe: Real or Imaginary?</u> 1972 Princeton, New Jersey, Princeton University press, p., 83

16   Merkl, p. 158

17   Ibid., p. 158

18   Ibid., p. 160

19   Ibid., p. 161

20   Ibid., p. 139

21   Korbel, p. 60

22   Merkl, p. 140

23   Ibid., p. 176

24   Harned, p. 18

25   U.S. Congress, House Committee on International Relations, Hearings before the Sub-committee on International Political and Military Affairs, presented by Arthur A. Hartmann, 94th Congress, 1st session, 1975, p. 18.

26   Ibid., p. 18

27   Merkl, p. 165

28   Povolny, p. 222

29   President Richard Nixon, <u>Address To Congress, May 1973</u>

30   Hassner, p. 12

31   Joseph M.A.H. Luns, "NATO View of Security Conferences", <u>Atlantic Community Quarterly</u>, Spring 1973, pp. 55-64, p. 60.

32   Kenneth Rush, "The NATO Alliance: The Basis for an Era of Negotiations", <u>Atlantic Community Quarterly</u>, Fall 1973, pp. 327-334, p. 331

33   Michael Debré, "The Defense of Europe and Security in Europe", <u>Atlantic Community Quarterly</u>, Spring 1973, pp. 93-118, pp. 116-117

34   Ibid., pp. 116-117

35   Hartmann, Frederick H., <u>The Relations of Nations</u>, New York: Macmillan Publishing Co., Inc., 1973 p. 16

36   Hassner, pp. 38-39

37   Kenneth Rush, "Address to the Southern Council for International and Public Affairs", <u>Department of State Bulletin</u>, June 18, 1973, pp. 867-871.

38   U.S. Secretary of State Rogers, <u>Foreign Policy Report</u>, April 19, 1973

39   Nils Andren, "European Security Conference: A Swedish Scholar's View", <u>Atlantic Community Quarterly</u>, Fall 1972, pp. 312-320, p. 316.

40   Griffiths, p. 22

41   Palmer, p. 16

42   Griffiths, p. 22

43   Povolny, p. 227

44   L. Radoux, rapporteur, <u>European Parliament Working Documents,</u> Doc. 485/74, On behalf of the Political Affairs Committee, February 21, 1974, p. 17fn.

45   Timothy Stanley and Darnell M Whitt, <u>Détente Diplomacy: United States and European Security in the 1970s</u>, 1970 New York, Dunellen Publishing Company, Inc., p. 90.

46   Palmer, p. 19

47   <u>European Parliament Working Documents</u>, Doc. 485/74. P. 23

48   Ibid., p. 23

49   Ibid., p. 24

50   Hartmann, p. 10

51   Flora Lewis, "Security Talks Moving to Finale", <u>New York Times</u>, February 18, 1975, p. 40.

52   Hartmann, p. 20

53   Ibid., p. 7

54   Ibid., p. 23

55   <u>European Parliament Working Documents</u>, Doc. 485/74. P. 30

56   Ibid., p. 27

57   Hartmann, P. 23

58   Rush, <u>Atlantic Community Quarterly</u>, p. 328

59   Griffiths, p. 22

60   Hassner, p. 20

61   Griffiths, p. 45

62   Ibid., p. 60

63   Hartman, p. 3

64   C.L. Sulzberger, "A Cold Peace for a Cold War", <u>New York Times</u>, August 4, 1972, p. 31 and December 5, 1972, p. 31.

65   "Issue of Advance Notice of Maneuvers Delaying European Security Conference", <u>New York Times</u>, June 29, 1975, p. 12

66   Flora Lewis, <u>New York Times</u>, February 28, 1975

67   David Binder, <u>New York Times</u>, June 10, 1975

68   <u>New York Times</u>, June 29, 1975

69   Hartmann, p. 17

70   <u>European Parliament Working Documents</u>, Doc. 485/74, p. 25

71   Harned, p. 25

72   Douglas G. Scrivner, "The Conference on Security and Cooperation in Europe: Implications for Soviet-American Détente", Spring 1976, <u>Denver Journal of International Law and Policy</u>, Vol. 6, No. 1, pp. 122-156, p. 130

73   Hartmann, p. 12

74   <u>Time</u>, January 31, 1977, p. 39

75   <u>European Parliament Working Documents</u>, Doc. 485/74, p. 31

76   Hartmann, p. 5

77   Ibid., p. 5

78   Ibid., p. 3

79   Ibid., p. 4

80   Scrivner, p. 137

81   Hartmann, p. 5

82   <u>New York Times</u>, August 3, 1975

83   <u>U.S. News and World Report</u>, June 6, 1977, p. 8

84   <u>Murray Seeger</u>, "Poland Lets Germans Migrate", <u>Los Angeles Times</u>, September 1976

85   <u>European Parliament Working Documents</u>, Doc. 485/74, p. 18

86   Hartmann, p. 5

87   Michael Getter, "Rights Issue Gives Helsinki Review Unexpected Role", <u>Washington Post</u>, March 17, 1977, p. A19

88   Luns, p. 63

89   Birnbaum, pp. 117-118

90   <u>Washington Post</u>, March 17, 1977, p. 19

Printed in the United States
By Bookmasters